IN RUSSIA

IN RUSSIA

INGE MORATH   ARTHUR MILLER

A STUDIO BOOK · THE VIKING PRESS · NEW YORK

ACKNOWLEDGMENTS

Basic Books, Inc.: "Leaves and Roots" by Andrei Voznesensky, translated by Stanley Kunitz, and lines from "Triptych" by Andrei Voznesensky, translated by Max Hayward, from *Antiworlds and the Fifth Ace* by Andrei Voznesensky, edited by Patricia Blake and Max Hayward, © 1966, 1967 by Basic Books, Inc., Publishers, New York.

Doubleday & Company, Inc.: "Bratsk Station" and "I Journeyed Through Russia," from *Bratsk Station and Other New Poems*, Copyright 1966 by Sun Books Pty Ltd, reprinted by permission of Doubleday & Company, Inc.

Hill & Wang, Inc.: from *Voznesensky: Selected Poems*, translated by Herbert Marshall, Copyright © 1966 by Herbert Marshall, used by permission of Hill & Wang, Inc.

Robert Lowell: "Stalin" and lines from "You and I Will Sit for a While in the Kitchen," adapted by Robert Lowell wth Olga Carlisle, Copyright © 1965 by Robert Lowell.

October House, Inc.: from "Second Dedication" by Andrey Voznesensky, from *The New Russian Poets 1953 to 1966*, selected, edited, and translated by George Reavey, Copyright © 1966 by George Reavey, reprinted by permission of October House, Inc.

Princeton University Press: from *Eugene Onegin*, translated from the Russian, with a commentary, by Vladimir Nabokov, Vol. 2, page 311, Bollingen Series LXXII (Copyright © 1964 by Bollingen Foundation). Pantheon Books now published by Princeton University Press.

Random House, Inc.: from *Two Centuries of Russian Verse*, Avrahm Yarmolinsky, editor, Copyright 1949, © 1962, 1965, 1966 by Avrahm Yarmolinsky, and from *Poets on Street Corners* by Olga Carlisle, © Copyright 1968 by Random House, Inc. Both reprinted by permission of Random House, Inc.

Rose Styron: from "The Mirror" by Boris Pasternak, adapted by Rose Styron with Olga Carlisle.

To Edgar and Mathilde Morath

I

It is now over fifty years since a relatively small radical party in Russia over-threw the government of the Czars and created the world's first socialist state. It has been half a century of comparisons as a result, for the Marxist claim from the beginning was that society could be run on a rational, scientific basis, thus opening an entirely novel chapter in man's struggle to govern himself. For the Westerner traveling in the Soviet Union, to see was to compare; here was the land in which the last would be first, and contrary to the West, the community rather than individual aggrandizement the high aim of education and society itself.

But the problem has always been, with what to compare? The American is especially torn by this because he is both the best and the worst observer of Soviet things. The best because the Soviet Union is at present the only country cast to the same physical scale as the United States in terms of its technological possibilities and resources; and the ideal standard of accomplishment in the Soviet mind itself is more often than not that of the United States. We are the worst observers, however, wherever we are face to face with poverty, inefficiency, or dirt. The moment we set foot abroad we forget that some of our cities are the dirtiest, worst kept in any "developed" country, our public transportation most abominable, our medical services for the poor close to horrible, and so forth. Instead, we compare the worst in Russia with the best in America. Food, for example. Nourishing though it is, most Russian food seems heavy and not very varied. There is some terrific food in New York, but between New York and Chicago, Chicago and St. Louis, St. Louis and San Francisco, is a gastronomic wasteland, and so it goes.

We are also the best and the worst when it comes to understanding what Russians are talking about—the language difficulty itself apart. We both share an absolute faith in progress, which is to say that man's fate is to go from worse to better, and we are as one in believing that the benefits of progress must be spread among all the people. So we are both very eager to know what a person "does," how much he makes, what sort of house he lives in. The Russian conversation, however, soon gropes toward fundamental attitudes, states of mind, the nature of the person rather than his occupation, and this is something we do not know how to talk about; it verges on "philosophy," which to most normally educated Americans is what history was to Henry Ford—"bunk." It is perhaps the basic reason why Chekhov, for example, is so hard to perform outside Russia, and especially difficult in the United States. To us, the characters seem vague, disconnected from one another, strangely abstract rather than real. We are much more interested in what a thing is, how it works, and very little interested in what it means. We are the triumph of technology. The irony is that the Russian aspires to hard, materialist, dialectically sound explanations of processes—the American style—when in fact he is extraordinarily quick to idealize and to reach for general principles. Nothing could be more alien to the American.

This book makes no attempt to compare Russia with any other place. It does not contrast the woman riveter with the chic mannequin, the new skyscraper with the old Russian log house. Neither is it a reportage of Russian progress or decay. It is bereft of political nationalism or cultural partisanship. It reports the images which underlie the Russian cultural consciousness—the images evoked by novels, poems, paintings, and plays and by their creators, and there is nothing that has more sweetness, more personal meaning for these people.

A few months before Ilya Ehrenburg's death Inge Morath and I spent an afternoon with him in his apartment talking of this remarkable sense of connection between Russians and their writers. On the way to his house we had passed an excavation for a new Moscow building, and a long line of dump trucks was waiting on the street to descend into the pit for loading. It must have been around zero Fahrenheit, which in Russia seems much colder than zero in New York. (There is a story of the Hungarian farmer who, just after the Second World War, came running into his hut in near hysteria, explaining to his wife that he had just seen two surveyors on his land marking off a new boundary. "They say our farm is going to be inside Russia!" he exclaimed. "So what?" his wife said. "It won't be any worse for us than in Hungary." "Yes," he cried, "but you can freeze to death in Russia!" The truth somewhere in that story is that the place often *looks* so much colder than it really is.) The trucks' windshields were all frosted over as the drivers waited, but one had its window opened an inch so that the glass was less fogged and I could see the man inside, his head and cheeks covered with a muskrat hat, thick gloves on his hands, and a quilted jacket giving him an enormous bulk. He was reading a book while he waited. I came closer and saw that it was in dialogue, a play.

The idea of a truck-driver reading a play was, to say the least, amazing. Ehrenburg had traveled the world and knew why foreigners made so much of this, and he said, "Yes, one thing we did do—we made readers of them."

But quite evidently he did not think this advance in literacy and interest in literature had resolved the questions of governing the Russians. He was in his seventies then, a man who had known many—hundreds, no doubt—who had been shot or simply disappeared, some of Russia's best writers and artists and journalists, of whose agony and fate he was one of the few living witnesses. For reasons no one is able quite to define, he was many times spared the very common fate. Some say he was an adept compromiser, others that it was a pure matter of luck that Stalin neglected to thumb him into the earth.

Perhaps he was already fatally ill; he was certainly incapable of any sign of joy. The Picassos on his walls, the sculpture all about, the perfectly French atmosphere—it was all somehow like a special room in a museum built to illustrate a style. This was no affectation with him, however; France was his love as it has been for cultivated Russians for a century. I had one strong memory connected to his name. At a certain point during the German invasion of Russia, when it had become clear that they might indeed lose the country to fascism, Ehrenburg had made a famous broadcast. Hate Germans, he had said. It was more than a traditional wartime cry. It meant that even if the Nazi armies were filled with the German working class, the old moral claims of international working-class solidarity were now cast down; the Soviet Union had become Russia again, as was inevitable, and class solidarity relegated to the closet of useless sentimental emotions.

I recall only his sadness that afternoon, little of what he said. Since then, I have read his memoirs, and now the reason is easy to understand. He had been up to his neck in the Spanish Civil War, which as he says was an upsurge of brotherhood reaching out into every nation. In Spain he had worked alongside other correspondents and writers, Soviet military men, fliers, advisers; returning to Russia in the midst of the Stalin purges, he found to his astonishment that many of these were being arrested, some shot, including the greater part of the officer corps of the Soviet Army itself. "There was no one in the circle of my acquaintances," he wrote, "who could be sure about the morrow; many of them kept a small suitcase with two changes of warm underwear permanently in readiness. Some of the tenants of the house in Lavrushensky Lane asked for the noisy lift to be out of action at night. It kept them awake, listening and wondering where it would stop. . . . In the office of *Izvestia* boards used to hang on the glass doors with the names of heads of departments, but now there was nothing; the messenger girl explained to me that it was not worth having them made: 'Here today and gone tomorrow.'"

A few short years later, the war came to Moscow, which had meanwhile joined hands with Hitler, the same Hitler whose troops and supplies had beaten the Spanish Loyalists. The war was won, and within a few more years Stalin was dead, and at least some of his crimes revealed by the party itself. Ehrenburg wrote: "After the Twentieth Party Congress, some of the people I met abroad asked me, as they also asked themselves, whether a mortal blow had not been dealt to the very idea of Communism. There is something here which they do not fully appreciate but which I, an old non-party writer, know: the idea proved so strong that it was Communists who were able to tell our people and the whole world about the past crimes, about the distortions both of the philosophy of Communism and of its principles of justice, solidarity and humanity. . . . The thought came to me that I should have to remain silent for a very long time . . . I should have no one with whom to share my experiences."

The *idea* remains but the blow "was dealt to the people of my generation. Some perished. Others will remember those years to their dying day."

Sitting there with him I could not help wondering why, even after he had known how uncertain survival was under Stalin, he had still chosen several times to return home from his trips abroad. Or why Madame Natasha Stoliarova, his secretary, whose tired and handsome face showed the depth of suffering in prisons over a period of years—why she, who continued to visit relatives in Switzerland and elsewhere, still chose to live in a place that must be alive with ghosts, not alone the ghosts of the unjustly punished but of high promises rudely smashed.

Clearly there is something, called Russia, which holds such people despite everything, a sort of grand maternity which enfolds and sometimes suffocates but is nevertheless as real as injustice and yet is ultimately beautiful, making other countries seem tame, superficial, irrelevant. I have never met cunning so naïve or naïveté so cunning. To feel at all here is to feel to the utmost. There were days when it seemed that apocalypse had been invented here, especially on the train ride from Germany to Moscow.

The snow-covered fields turn into a white sea, hour after hour after hour— it is a night and a day from the European border to Moscow—until a kind of speech or song emerges from its boundlessness. The idea of Napoleon and Hitler that human beings from Europe could cross this ocean and live to conquer Moscow is truly insane, like the delusions of a maniac who fills his lungs with air, hoping to soar to the moon. To fight in that boundless snow, to sit crouching in it at night, to keep hope alive in that wind . . . Even to a foreigner at a train window the Russian earth is crammed with the dead and the wild visions of armies drawn toward that silent mother who devours.

There is a tenderness toward what is Russian even in those whom she has punished, even in those who live part of their psychic lives in unrelieved fury at official hypocrisy and bureaucratic stupidity. In person after person one finds, below the political hostility toward so much that goes on, a feeling we would probably call patriotism but which is really a helpless kind of belonging. Madame Mandelshtam, widow of a great poet whom in 1934 she followed into exile—where he died after a second condemnation in 1938—seems to have clawed her way up to a kind of spiritual equilibrium, an outspoken contempt for everything superficial, whether it be a literary evaluation or the latest pronouncement of a high official, but enriched by a suffering which forbids easy cures and solutions. One inevitably expects her to make an invidious comparison of Russian practice with the West, but the West's attitudes are very nearly beside the point for such as she. Just when one expects her to make a comparison she says, instead, "You must remember what these people have suffered. The sufferings of the Russian people are incomparable."

It was as though she did not wish Russia corrected by those who, with the best will in the world, had not shared the Russian experience and did not hold in their hearts the depth of love and hatred which profound suffering leaves in its victims. Talking with her it suddenly seemed we were no longer talking politics or sociology or perhaps even history. It is as though both oppressors and victims had been driven by the fullness of their humanity, by an often brutal surge toward ultimate meanings. With her, as with many others on both sides of past and current repressions, one cannot avoid remembering Dostoevsky's conception of Russia as being fated to lead mankind to salvation. It is not, however, quite the same thing as American or British salvationism; for them this is not a question of law and order, or of raising the standard of living of their own and other peoples they have gone abroad to "protect."

I was passing under the Kremlin wall one winter afternoon and said in an idle, musing way to a Russian friend, "There must have been some goings-on in there the day they decided to get rid of Khrushchev." He looked at me in surprise and said, "We don't bother with what happens in there. They know what they are doing." There was even a trace of pride in his tone, a declaration of personal faith and security. And even people who see clearly that all is not well often seem to desire that this same pyramidal structure remain undisturbed. It is as though there were an anarchy in the center of their beings which, left to itself, would expand to a dematerialization of all order. And more and more Americans are coming to understand the seeming reasonableness of such a feeling as they buy more and more guns and suspect that under certain conditions the center will not hold.

In a time of trouble, when all the solutions are blocked, men must believe that someone knows what to do, and the thought is intolerable that those above are foundering just like those below. Russia for a hundred years has been in an uninterrupted time of trouble, and the will to believe is called up from the depths quite as powerfully as the doubt that anything is believable.

An interpreter, a woman so kind, so sentimental, that instead of translating for me at a performance of Andrei Voznesensky's "The Triangular Pear" she simply sat there shaking her head and weeping, and when I asked for a clue as to what was being said, looked up at me apologetically and whispered, "Oh, it's so beautiful!"—this woman had been to the United States several times and admires much of it, but once she asked, "With everybody in America pursuing his own interests, how do you hold it all together?"

A good question. My only answer was, "How do you hold this together with everybody directed by such a handful of people? That's much harder, isn't it?" We were both left with the questions unanswered, but I thought again that she sensed a centrifugal force in herself and the Russians which, left to itself, could only send everything flying off into space. And who knows, after all, how long the eighteenth-century concept of the individual which the American Constitution and the Bill of Rights enshrine can endure in an age which increasingly organizes from above every act and feeling of man? "The pursuit of happiness," the individual thrust toward a private fate, was never the Russian idea, nor indeed that of most of the world. The Communists did not invent the idea of "the People," they merely moved it a few inches under a Marxist heading, a counter in the universal dialectic of the class struggle. It was not Khrushchev who invented a contempt for art that is considered abstract, personal, and meaningless to the masses; it was Tolstoy, one of the world's few real individualists, who saw in the painting on the side of a peasant's cart greater glory than in all the deliberate sophisticated art in the capitals of Europe. "The People" is the measure of all things, not the person, and perhaps we in America fear this most because we understand it best in our blood. Truman at the piano did not play Stravinsky or Aaron Copland but "The Missouri Waltz," and Eisenhower read cowboy stories, not *Moby Dick*. A cultural adviser like André Malraux might seem perfectly natural in France but not in Russia and not in America, the two societies in all the world attempting to arrive at classlessness, and the two most racked in their spirit by the hypocritical class contradictions in their social lives. The abyss between the reality at hand and the dream of classlessness, between what exists and justice, is the bottomless gorge into which we throw our lies. Until one day the hole fills up.

In Georgia one day I asked a professional man about class in Russia. Georgia is like the mountain areas of Southern California, with rain; or northern California, with sunshine. You can go into high mountains in Georgia without passing a timberline, and grapes grow in the clouds. There is a juiciness in the earth itself, an inexhaustible presentation of melons and ruins. I had noticed, not only in Tbilisi but everywhere in Russia, that ordinary policemen almost always came to attention and saluted when any big car went by, especially if the shades were drawn, and more especially if the rear window was covered by a pleated curtain. The day before, this man, a university teacher, had been run into by another motorist who had smashed his car's taillight. He was now generating the energy to find another taillight and a mechanic to install it. (There is no car insurance—you simply work things out impromptu between yourself and the other party as to who pays for what.) But, said he, for people of influence and position, everything is available. More, these important people can get away with anything as regards the law.

I expected some monstrous example. "Supposing I break some traffic regulation, or even have an accident which is my fault. If I am a party man, or have connections, the police will look the other way. If I don't, I am in trouble." And then, poor man, he turned his sincere eyes to me and said, "Not like in America. You are all treated the same by the police in America." Misery loves hope, I thought.

II

Inge Morath and I traveled together through most of the places pictured in this book, but it is only now that I realize she took no photographs of turbines, dams, construction projects, or the other usual scenes that attract foreign cameras in Russia. An "objective" photo-report would have to include, and probably concentrate on, Russian scientific accomplishments, but in truth what is shown in this book is what one feels in the country, and it is probably what lies imbedded in the minds of the people, rather than the images of the oil-cracking plant, the machine shop, and the new hotel. More, the distinctive Russian style is indeed something that seems old-fashioned to many of us.

There certainly are thousands of housing projects, blocks of new flats little different from their counterparts around London, New York, or Paris—the true international style of anonymous uniform cubes which surely will be torn down one great day when the world has built sufficient shelter for everyone and can begin to construct human habitations. Moscow has radial avenues of new Grand-Concourse-type apartment houses as depressing as New York's until one is told by a resident how delightful it is to live alone in an apartment instead of sharing a hard-to-heat log house with several other families. The Russian housing project is roughly finished inside compared to ours, but on the other hand it is surrounded in winter by hundreds of children and adults skiing. A few blocks away, it might be added, the old log houses remain, and there are women on a frozen pond washing clothes through a hole in the ice.

There are, of course, terribly clean subways, reliable aircraft connecting every part of the country, some excellent trains, first-class science laboratories, and the rest. But underneath the sheet aluminum and the modern design there is the indigenous nationality of feeling which is not modern at all if modernity means what is happening in the West these days. And why should it be otherwise, when most people in Russia work on the land, and the city folk, in so many cases, are peasant stock once-removed? As I walked down a city street, it often seemed to me that not only what we think of as modernity but also the city itself in Russia is an implanted thing, and that the urban man who has created the civilizations of the West is still in the making here. His habitual loneliness, his totally private life, his ignorance of his neighbors, his go-it-alone psychology—these are still in conflict in Russia with an older way of communal existence. There is no real analogy in America and even less in Europe, where the city is ancient and its powers of rulership long since digested, but we can still look back to something similar in the America of before World War I, when the cities were filling up with country people who had to learn to be up-to-date—to forget the ideas of mutual help, for instance, and to relate themselves to an impersonal administration rather than to officials they knew and to personalities they understood and who understood them. There is still a homeliness about many Russians that has the scent of the country in it, a capacity for welcoming strangers with open, unabashed curiosity, a willingness to show feeling, and above all a carelessness about the passing of time.

This country root is naturally the enemy of efficiency and in the long run will probably disappear, but it seems to explain otherwise incomprehensible contradictions in the Russian spiritual landscape. One afternoon, for example, I was sitting on the ground floor of a building belonging to the Writers' Union with five or six Russian writers, when I noticed a gigantic figure just outside the French windows, a person big to begin with but enlarged by a quilted coat and immense felt boots. The conversation within revolved around literature and publishing; outside, this person was digging a ditch in the frozen earth and casting shovelfuls of ice onto a growing pile. Suddenly I realized this was a woman, a woman stabbing a space into that stubborn ground in cold that made it hard to breathe. I said, gesturing toward the window, that it was a pretty cold day to be digging. The others barely glanced at her and went on with the conversation. They did not seem particularly heartless men, and of course most of the people who load snow onto trucks to clear the streets are women. It is even possible that they would defend the use of women for such work on grounds of sexual equality, but this particular woman was, it seemed to me, particularly peasantlike, immense, wide-faced, ruddy, and the peasant woman, like the farm woman in any country, is naturally a physical laborer. With the subway gleaming underground and immense modern buildings rising all around us, this woman digging a ditch in such frightfully cold weather while socially conscious writers in a warm room spoke in perfect ease of spiritual matters—one knows at such moments that historic Russia is not yet dead.

So in a strict sense it is not always a pure question of injustice that is involved here, or even of insensitivity to suffering. Surely an American has little right to a claim of high sensitivity in such matters given, as one instance, the Negro's conditions of life, which leave most whites unmoved. Certain settings are natural, handed down by history, and only become unnatural when the diggers find a way to make trouble. What is strange, however—and some of these photographs embody that strangeness—is the Russian attitude toward artists, and the concomitant attitude toward community itself.

Russia is the only country I know of where one writer will passionately extol the works of a competitor. This is rather a shock at first and nearly unbelievable—and indeed, in some cases it is merely politic, but it happens genuinely often enough to force one to think about it. Of course in my presence they are talking to a foreigner, but that is just the point: in any other country the ignorant foreigner is usually sold on the unique excellence of the writer he happens to be speaking to at the moment—there is never much else of value. And in Russia it is also true that the more acclaim the writer has earned, the more he is at pains to draw one's attention to others less renowned but equally talented.

It is otherwise in France, England, Germany, or the United States, and it seems at first like a pure generosity of spirit, which it may well be, but it is also mildly tactical as well. There is a deep division among Soviet writers which reflects two conflicting attitudes toward power itself. As in any other country, the majority is not about to get in the way of the powerful. Most writers, like most other people, know where their bread is buttered. But there is also a minority in league with the future, the growing tip of the tree, and a certain amount of danger is always at their side. This is one of the reasons why both kinds of writer—although the vanguard is more likely to do this— will direct attention to colleagues of the same persuasion. It is a kind of politicking, a way of strengthening the side.

But what exactly are both factions after, what—beyond the obvious advantages of supporting the regime—are the so-called conservatives aiming at in their works, and what in the vanguard enrages them so?

The obvious answers are ideological, but they are not altogether explanatory. The conservative writer sees himself in the tradition of the realistic work of Tolstoy, for example—although he will disassociate himself from the master's mysticism and religiosity. Art, he would say, is basically the higher consciousness of the people, immediately comprehensible to them, and an enhancement of the values of socialism. Socialism is the Soviet system, whose fundamental objectives are humane, progressive, and generally directed toward the welfare of all. In a word, art is like science, a servant of the community. In fact, the whole concept is Platonic and by no means uniquely Russian or even Communist.

The Puritan fathers of the Massachusetts Bay Colony, for instance, would not have countenanced novels and poems which unearthed the sexual repressions enforced by their semi-military discipline, let alone advocated freer sexuality. The colony was always in danger and a man who kept himself apart from its spiritual defense, a man who deeply questioned the underlying propositions of the society, would not and did not last very long. The famed Roger Williams objected too strongly to the theocratic suppression of variant religious ideas, and on top of that preached the equality in spirit of the Indians whom the white men were deceiving and robbing—and was promptly put out in the dead of winter to die. It was the Indians who saved him, and in Rhode Island he set up the first society on the American continent where the freedom to think was guaranteed.

The conservative Russian writer—the honest one anyway—is moved by the fear that the high communal aims of the Communist state will be atomized, diluted, and ultimately destroyed by the individualistic vanguard. But the writer who feels this way also has attitudes, apparently little connected with ideology, which also place him firmly in this ideological camp. He is more than likely, for example, to enjoy the feeling of solidarity with the party, with workers, and with other non-writers whose reality he shares. He is another kind of worker and takes pride in it, a worker in literature or art. It is not onerous but a matter of duty and goodness to accept party revisions of his work. He is likely to emphasize the virtues of craftsmanship, solid construction, and thoroughness in a work of art. He wants, in short, to be part of what-is. He is rationalist in his explanation of man.

It needs to be said that many of these men, like their counterparts everywhere, have been neither suborned nor corrupted by superior force. Accepting the fundamental bases of Soviet society, they honestly regard what injustice they see as temporary error or at worst a lamentable necessity which does not prove the rule. They are men who desire authority and fear chaos. For them life can never be tragic because the individual who comes to a bad end has simply separated himself from the victorious path of the society. Stalin stated their viewpoint most aptly—the writer is the engineer of the soul. Rather than speaking truth to power, he justifies power to the people. His greatest justification is quite probably the career and works of Mikhail Sholokhov, whose trilogy of the Russian Civil War in the Don Cossack area seems to demonstrate that art and absolute fealty to the state can be combined without damage.

There are those, on the other hand, who point out that Sholokhov revised his masterwork to minimize the values of those Cossacks who opposed the Red Army, and so weakened his achievement. Some even suggest that Sholokhov did not write these works but stood in as the author while the real author was liquidated. This last, however, seems unlikely as new Sholokhov stories have recently appeared and their style is the same as the works of thirty years ago. But the imputation indicates the depth of bitterness between the two factions. Sholokhov is a raunchy old Cossack now, advocating that the whipper-snappers be fed to the sharks if they don't like the way things are in the Soviet Union. His identification, in all likelihood, is with those first heroic revolutionaries who stood up like men before the Czar's agents and firing squads, and despite unimaginable deprivation, betrayals, and hardships, dragged Russia out of feudalism and into the age of science and modernity. To a Sholokhov, the power he respects and upholds is the power that fends off the decadence of the West—the pornography, the effeminacy, the rootless, nationless, cryptic, private art whose supremacy anywhere means the end of community itself. There are millions of Sholokhovs everywhere, needless to say, the difference being that in the Soviet Union a writer is far more than an individual facing a piece of blank paper alone in a room; he is state property and accountable for his attitudes. But as revolutionary ideas move into the streets in the West, much the same sort of conflict is rising among writers there. A LeRoi Jones, committed to black militancy, has no patience with Negro writers whose work does not forward the cause, and he would surely regard as an enemy and betrayer a talented Negro who spent his time dealing with matters irrelevant to that cause. Any claim to the autonomy of art must collapse when a people is in danger or struggling to preserve itself, and the single theme of Soviet political and social discourse for half a century has been its imminent peril before foreign and domestic enemies. Actually, much the same emotions work inside us. Until very recently it was a rare Hollywood movie that ventured to question any basic American social premise, and the studio heads exercised an ironbound censorship of any such story. They were avowedly providing "wholesome" entertainment in which fundamental con-servative American ideas always emerged victorious—or at a minimum were awarded a metaphoric justification. School boards all over the country screen out material from textbooks they deem subversive of national values, whatever the validity of that material, and on the most blatant level the House Un-Ameri-can Activities Committee for more than thirty years has arraigned writers and others whom it regards as dangerous to accepted thinking. Among other questions asked me by the chairman of that committee was, "Why do you write so sadly about this country?" It is a truly Stalinist question, if you will, and there are millions of Americans who share the chairman's feelings. Given the right political atmosphere, the kind we had in the 1950s, these deeply angry people will come out on the streets to picket movies and plays by authors they regard as hostile to American values, and given the legal power would unquestionably clean up our literary production in a matter of weeks.

The difference, therefore, is not in the uniqueness of Russian feelings toward such matters but in the legal systems; all Russian literature is published by the state and must meet the requirements of the Communist Party. That a certain number of works have been published which criticize or imply that all is not on the right track, indicates that within the party are men who have come to recognize that the role of the writer may not be quite as simple as Stalin thought. Obviously some of them see that the writer's criticisms might even strengthen the state by bringing to light real shortcomings which ought not be continually rationalized away. There are even a few who understand that the heavy censorship has bled much of Soviet writing of its individuality and sheer interest.

It is not possible to begin to understand anything about the feelings of either young or old Soviet artists without keeping in mind Ehrenburg's admission— "The thought came to me that I should have to remain silent for a very long time . . . I should have no one with whom to share my experiences."

Nothing is easier than to read a bad conscience into this, and little more; he should have fled when he could, or spoken out against what he knew was wrong, and so forth. But there is something much more. It is a little like a man trying to explain how he fell in love with a perfect woman who turned out to be murderous, vain, even insane, and cared nothing for him, a woman to whom he had dedicated his works, his life, and his highest idealistic feelings. How can you explain that, when the truth is now so obvious to your listener? It is impossible spiritually to tear oneself apart from a beloved without leaving a part of yourself behind, and the Soviet scene is still under the tension of of this same paradox, even in the hearts of those too young to have been touched by Stalinism. For the power of the Communist ideal is on the level of the religious one, of any belief in sacrifice to a higher and worthier ideal than one's own selfish interests.

And that is why so many of the Ehrenburg generation, any of those who once felt the totality of belief, seem so saddened now regardless of the fact that some, at least, of the truth of Stalinism has been revealed and its excesses curbed—most of the time, anyway.

Konstantin Simonov is in his fifties now. He is the author of good, workable plays, poems, and novels, and during the war was a front-line correspondent who saw more action than a great many soldiers. His line of communication to the highest levels of the party is still open. He lives very well, sometimes in a spacious Moscow apartment, sometimes in a country house where the shelves are littered with icons, sculpture, and paintings from Russia and from the many other countries he has visited. The sentencing of Yuri Daniel to prison he does not agree with; Daniel was a soldier and wounded at that. Sinyavsky is another story, for he never served in the war, and worse, perhaps, knowingly had his manuscripts published abroad rather than standing up for them at home and struggling to get them accepted. Still, Simonov can swallow his resentment of Sinyavsky too, knowing that it was not intelligent, by even putting him on trial, to give the world a club with which to beat the Soviet Union. Simonov is caught, it seems, between a certain sense of honor, which to him Sinyavsky violated, and the hard-learned lesson that imprisonment is no longer the answer to literary dissidence.

At the same time Simonov will not forgo any chance to put down bad writers, whatever their loyalty, or foreign partisans of the Soviet whose works are empty. In short, he seems to have arrived at substantive rather than relative values. And inevitably, his journals of the war, a work he regards as perhaps the most important of his career, have been refused publication for several years now. But apparently he is determined to think and work within the slowly changing system and to fight the battle as he can.

Simonov may still be *persona grata* with the regime but he is at bottom a working writer and knows that censorship finally means an instruction to writers to lie. A patriot, as Russian as you can get and still stay sober, he has that double vision of his country which the awakened live with; he often seems nearly ashamed of what is still done in the name of national security and socialist truth. But he is not an official, and I wanted to hear the official attitude toward writers and censorship. There were two opportunities.

Madame Ekaterina Furtseva is the nominal chief of all cultural work in the Soviet Union. We met in her office, a long and impressive room with a green felt-covered table in the center surrounded by armchairs, and a working desk at one end beneath two tall windows. Behind the chair was a ten-foot-long table piled high with possibly two hundred manuscripts and books. Slips of paper stuck out of those books and manuscripts—indicating, I assumed, marked passages.

Madame Furtseva was then in her sixties, a sensitive and still handsome woman, attentive and intelligent. Suffering had carved deeply into her face. Indeed, one day a few years ago, in the midst of a business meeting, a man in working clothes had entered her office and with a pair of clippers cut the wire of the phone that connected her office directly with Khrushchev's. She went home and slashed her wrists. Having been raised under Stalin, she knew what this gesture must mean. She was saved, however, and Khrushchev ordered her restored to her position, for she had been a favorite of his. When it is said that Russia has not really changed much one must keep in mind that "much" can sometimes mean everything. But what such an incident still leaves in the mind of the foreigner is that the restoration is still quite as arbitrary and unpredictable as the condemnation, resting on a leader's temperament rather than on legally secured rights.

I knew that writers rather liked her—all sorts of writers, conservative and vanguard alike, more or less. The general feeling was that she cared about literature and was basically humane, and was not simply a police agent in disguise. Four or five officials sat around the table, she at the head. These were chiefs of various departments, one in charge of theater, another of children's books, and so on. They said nothing and were clearly of a lower but still considerable rank. They wore dark, well-pressed suits, starched collars, and subdued ties. We might well have been in a bank, discussing a mortgage.

Madame Furtseva, arranging her long shawl over her shoulders, talked of the weather, of all our children, of plays she had seen—including my own. *A View from the Bridge* had been playing for a long time and I told her I had seen it the night before. She was immediately curious about my reaction to the production. I said that I thought some of the actors superb, but that certain excisions and changes in the script disturbed me. She was genuinely surprised at this—and as her office was in charge of translations, her responsibility was now on the agenda.

I went on to say that all the psychological motivation had been carefully removed from the play. Eddie Carbone, the hero, must *slowly* reveal an illicit attachment to his niece, a love which helps to move him toward a betrayal of his two brothers-in-law, who are illegal Sicilian immigrants. But in the Soviet version he has hardly entered the scene when he speaks of his love for his niece and whenever she appears he puts on an agony of frustration which makes any later revelation immaterial and foolish. One wondered why his wife remained in the house at all.

There were many other changes of the same sort—nothing is left to be developed and discovered, everything is stated at the outset, and rather crudely at that. I could not understand why the play was such a success.

Madame Furtseva was obviously appalled. She wanted to know from her assistants who had translated the play and why this had been allowed to happen. The matter would be looked into. Her sincerity emboldened me and I asked what the procedure was for selecting translators. To my astonishment she was quite vague about it. Not secretive, but genuinely vague, and even asked her assistants to help out with an explanation. The embarrassment now spread down the table. It turned out that translators in effect selected themselves; someone with a bit of English might hear of a foreign hit, get hold of a manuscript or a book, rush through a Russian version, and be the first to get to one of the Moscow or Leningrad theaters with a script. This, I said, sounded like arrant free enterprise, the rewards going not to the most able but to the most aggressive. We all had a good hollow laugh at this, but the problem remained.

After about an hour it seemed time to break up, and I said I did not want to keep her from her work any longer. She glanced behind her at the massive piles of books and manuscripts which awaited her perusal. Yes, she said, there was a vast amount of work to do. I asked if she had to read all those manuscripts and she said yes, she did have to; unfortunately it was necessary. What do you suppose would happen, I asked, if she just chucked it and didn't read them? Just let them go through. Would it really rock the country?

She laughed then, and I thought I detected a certain understanding in her laugh—as though the relaxation of censorship, even its abolition, had been discussed by her before this. I persisted; I had met some writers who were suspect to one degree or another, but their complaint was that the current system was not Communist enough rather than too Communist. As for Russia itself, their eyes melted at the mention of it. She nodded. She understood perfectly well. She knew it better than I did, I thought then.

Perhaps I was too taken with her and let myself read too much into that laugh—a certain recognition of at least a grain of absurdity in her exhausting attempts to keep the national mind loyal and clean and unquestioning. More, I thought at that moment that somewhere in her was the wish that the gates could open and that mistaken literature could be condemned by the people in their wisdom. But I could be wrong. I could also be right, however.

Two days later at a cocktail party one of her assistants sought me out. He handed me an envelope. It contained a chit for royalties due me on a story of mine which had been published in Moscow years before. I asked what this amount represented—was it all I was owed? He asked if I wanted more, the way you ask a guest if he wants more pickles. I said no, I wasn't here to dun them for royalties but was merely curious, although anything would be gratefully received. He then gave me the message which was obviously his chief business. Madame Furtseva had not spoken idly during our meeting; she wanted to assure me that she would personally see to it that from now on my translators would be the best that could be found. I thanked him. Then I asked, what about the translators for the other Americans they published and produced? He seemed taken aback, surprised; there had been no discussion of the others, or of the whole procedure of selecting translators. In short, this was irrelevant.

Perhaps I read too much into his reaction, but it seemed rather a harking back to the royal past. Rules applied to everyone excepting to those especially favored from on high, and his total and naïve acceptance of such a benign procedure was noteworthy, I thought—he saw nothing whatever unjust about it. I had earned a favor and would receive it. What could be better than that?

And yet—don't politicians do favors in Washington? Of course they do, but one imagines they are remotely ashamed. Perhaps one ought not imagine too much. Or is the moral simply that we are still laboring under some fringe of the old illusion which the great October Revolution raised before the world—that a government of and by the insulted and injured had finally risen on the earth, a society which had somehow abolished the motivations for immorality, the incarnation at long last of the human community. So that infractions here, any appearance of the Old Adam, are doubly scandalous, immensely more meaningful than anywhere else.

And that is one of the things I tried to tell two high officials of the Writers' Union, on another occasion, when one of them—call him apparatchik Leo—complained that writers in Spain, France, America, might be prosecuted but little was made of it, while the same thing in the Soviet Union had the whole world in an uproar. Leo, actually a professor rather than a writer, is a conservative in the Writers' Union, some would say a badly reformed Stalinist. His view is that foreign protests are basically made in bad faith; that in truth the protestors are more interested in making political capital against Communism than in gaining freedom for writers. I replied that this was undoubtedly true in many cases, but not in all by any means. The fact is that the Soviet Union has set itself up as an exemplar, the road to the future; that it has immense power to influence the future, and consequently what happens to freedom in Russia will inevitably have an impact on what happens to it elsewhere, just as such shifts of attitude inside the United States are of much greater import than in other, less powerful nations.

Thus we were led to discussing his attitudes toward censorship itself. You mean, he asked, that we should permit publication of *anything*? And he smiled at me incredulously, but there was also a kind of amused alarm in his eyes, quite as though I were insane or vaguely dangerous. I had been asked that same question once before, by a Cincinnati Congressman on the Un-American Activities Committee, and in both cases when I answered yes, I received the same look. But with Leo, if only because I was not about to be indicted for what I said, and sentenced to a year in jail, it was possible both to understand the nature of his feeling from past experience, and to speak to his feeling rather than simply to his armored ideology.

The writers you distrust so are not unpatriotic, I said. I have never known such love of country in any literary men. You are burdening your own talents with a backbreaking load of suspicion which, if it were removed, would quite likely open your country to a renaissance. The only other place where so much talent exists is in the United States. Let the people decide, at least to a far greater degree than they are allowed to now, what is valuable to them and what is destructive. You are far too great a nation to be descending to this ignoble hounding, this endless politics of suppression, liberation, and suppression again. These men are really not trying to overthrow Soviet society but to bring it closer to its own ideals. And so forth.

His reply was not only unexpected but, I thought, devastating. You mean we should spend the people's money publishing the pornography I have seen on your newsstands, books which interest young people in dope addiction, plays which espouse homosexuality, paintings which even your own critics admit are made only for publicity and money? All this, you are telling me, will be an improvement for Russia? We do not consider that an improvement. As he spoke I could hear the Knights of Columbus applauding, as well as many a member of the PTA, the United States Congress—and, quite frankly, myself to a degree, for the open pandering that goes on in the West for money gain is the worst advertisement for a free literature which that ragged cause has ever had to endure.

I could only answer that the presence of this stuff was the price one paid, but that the principle itself could not be discarded because of its abuse. It was, of course, an unacceptable rejoinder, and he knew it was and this made him happy. And I had to remind myself again that under this rubric of morality he was also content to keep out of print whatever serious works embodied the honest response of the people to the system. As protectors of the wholesome, his kind had the power to condemn as dishonest, perverted, and reactionary some of the finest work being written in the Soviet Union. And worse, this power to condemn was the power to elevate into importance hacks and non-writers whose claim to prominence was really their fealty to whatever the party had decided was correct. It was an unwholesome wholesomeness finally, a motivation toward bitterness and mean ungenerosity which revealed itself when we began speaking of those Russian writers who had been so acclaimed recently during their visits to the West. I had mentioned the poets Yevtushenko and Voznesensky as examples of the West's being prepared to open its arms to Soviet writers.

But, said Leo, you only open your arms to writers who criticize our system.

Not at all, I said; if Sholokhov came West he would find a great audience for his readings. But it is true that most of your writers who simply support the system would have a smaller audience, but that is because we expect writers to speak from their own souls, not from a political program. After all, you also welcome writers most who criticize their systems. It's because of the political advantage, but it is also that they are more likely to be speaking personally, rather than as ambassadors. Your poets, I went on, made a great impression because we were able to hear what a human being makes of life in Russia, aside from the intrinsic value of their works.

This theme, the travels of certain Russian writers, clearly interested, and I thought even angered, him. So he smiled. And what, he asked, did the Americans make of Voznesensky? A real neurotic, eh?

He went on in this vein—laughing in a condescending way, what you might call an established way, at these young poets who had written hardly enough even to warrent serious academic analysis, who showed off before foreigners, wearing all sorts of crazy clothes which they picked up in Paris or London, who were headlined in newspapers, quoted on radio and television, talked of as though they were geniuses, immortals. Suddenly the simplest truth hung shimmering before the blond, blue-eyed, rather Scandinavian Leo head—he was a professor who had worked so hard with little public recognition and no international acclaim, and along come these snotnoses and the whole world bandies their idiotic, unscannable verses, and veritable hordes of students worship their names. The evident frustration as he spoke of these neurotics, these show-offs, was, I thought, the same thing I had met a hundred times in American universities where professors had to face the fact that massive sums went to mere fictionalists and so little to those who bend their backs for years over the substantial studies of literature, the scholarship which nobody ever hears of. The difference, of course, is that those professors haven't the political and legal power literally to rule out of existence what irritates them.

I said that to Leo—that finally it came down to power. Censorship, the whole conception of an illegal literature, handed the power to suppress to individuals who might not be worthy of it, might use it to express their own narrowness of vision, and surely a country did not benefit from this.

And for the first time that afternoon a Russian said yes to an argument of mine. It came from the other official of the Writer's Union, who had sat quietly all this time. He was—call him apparatchik Ivan—a burly, gray-haired, tank-commander type, who can fracture a spine with a welcoming embrace. At a sad story, he weeps, at a glad one, blushes with pleasure. Once he had said to me, At the end of the war I got out of my tank and I looked up at the sky and I thought—now there are no more evil people in the world!

It was no idle remark. Now in his late sixties, he is of that generation whose lives were built around Hitler and the German threat. Through the fifteen years of his prime, from the early thirties to the end of the war in 1945, the defense not only of socialism but of Russia itself was the central spine of existence, and any measure that purported to strike at fascism was acceptable and good. During the war Ivan made his name writing militant, patriotic poetry which was widely respected. Afterward he became a power in the Writers' Union, and until Stalin's death presided over the destruction of many writers marked by the secret police as dangerous.

But even those who hate all that, writers and relatives and friends of the condemned, do not growl at his name but rather lament him. He did usher writers into the prison camps, but privately, when he could, he would slip money to an imprisoned writer's wife or secretly do what was possible to help mitigate punishments. Not much to say for a man, but not nothing either, given the risk involved.

Now, retired from his post, he is regarded as an irrelevant grandpa, a rather benign relic of a terrible time. I have seen him, in Yugoslavia, around a table with Yugoslavs his age, old partisan poet-fighters from the forties, drinking wine and bellowing at each other, pounding the table, hugging one another when a moving sentiment was uttered, singing the war songs as though invisible lines of troops were again behind them, and swearing faith in the human race.

He is a sentimentalist, a believer. The poetry of a Mandelshtam, a Voznesensky, however much he might respect it, is strange and unnerving in its questioning of all experience, its want of affirmation, its apolitical fascination with love, identity, and the evanescence of existence. He knows he is not with it any more, however, and, as he did with Leo and me during this discussion, he would like to mediate, to hold back any final condemnation of the West and its idea of freedom and at the same time to make me understand the mind of apparatchik Leo. Now, after the apocalypse, he seems to desire some tide of sheer good will through which America and Russia might submerge their hostility, rather than a principled confrontation which he knows can never, as such, resolve itself peacefully.

As we were about to part, a bright idea suddenly struck me. I said, you know, just after the American Revolution, Congress passed the Alien and Sedition Acts, which forbade publishing viewpoints opposed to the administration. Actually writers and printers were jailed and presses destroyed.

This was real news, I was glad to see. Both apparatchik Leo and apparatchik Ivan came to alert, even happy attention now. They understood this kind of thing. I laid it on even more; there was a widespread fear that enemies of the Revolution were trying to stir the people up. All kinds of very stringent orders were carried out against hostile opinions. They nodded. They truly understood.

Then, I went on, Thomas Jefferson was elected and threw out the whole business. It was never tried again. And mind you, I said, we were a very weak country then. And yet they decided to take their chances with the faith and good sense of the people.

Ivan quickly replied, "Yes, but by then they had already gotten rid of the English!" And he laughed heartily.

In other words, Russia was still insecure, the prey of spies, of the international bourgeoisie. But he did laugh. And once they had left my hotel room I looked around at the walls and up at the ceiling where the bug must be hidden, wondering if both these men had really been addressing it all along rather than me alone, rather than the issues, which perhaps they understood quite as well as anyone.

III

Thumbing through these pictures now brings back the ever-present sense of Russia's sheer massiveness, its scale, the feeling one never loses there, especially in wintertime, of a prehistoric, half-slumbering beast which one never knows how to approach when its great arms may either stroke one's cheek or squash one's body altogether. To the eye, if not to one's associations, there is something of London in Moscow's architecture. Not the style but the gray intention of remaining forever and changing only when it must.

Every weekday without fail a line of people appears waiting to enter the Lenin Mausoleum. Blond Russians, people with Mongol features, short men from God knows what desert five thousand miles away, patient in the biting wind, moving inch by inch toward the sepulcher of what can only be called a god. But then, just as one is sure that the twentieth century and its skepticism, its total overthrow of all ritual, is still being held back at the European border, a question flashes up out of an odd piece of behavior. There in line stood a Mongolian Red Army officer and his girl or wife. Enduring the icy air without flinching, their slant eyes expressionless, they stood a quarter-mile from the tomb in silence. She was dressed in a short fur coat and a big hat of red fox, her rubber boots had curved tops ending just at mid-calf. A strangely chic and sexy emanation from the changeless East. Suddenly she started to snap her fingers rhythmically, holding them out in front of her, and then did a series of rock-and-roll steps to get warm. The officer looked at her, laughed—a real New York laugh—and joined her by snapping his fingers to the same beat. Then they subsided and went on waiting to see Lenin.

Having managed to travel in Russia without official sponsorship and at our own expense, we could refuse guided tours, but the invitation to come to the State Horse Farm was too good to turn down. I knew they had troikas there, and the single greatest mystery to me from my first walk on a Russian street in winter was how people had managed to stay alive in an open sleigh in such cold. Every nineteenth-century Russian novel has rides across the fields in sleighs—I thought of Chekhov's trip to Sakhalin, Gogol's almost human troikas, Dostoevsky's characters' crazy flights over the snow, Tolstoy. Ten, twenty, thirty below zero in an open sleigh, for hours, too—how was it possible?

The manager of the farm is a larger version of Khrushchev. Immense hands, an open, friendly face, barrel-chested—obviously no horse would dare disobey him. Nor do they. We stand in an indoor ring from which corridors of stalls radiate. Everything whitewashed and clean, a proper environment for Soviet race horses, some of which American and European breeders are eager to buy, and often do. But Inge Morath, polite as ever, makes the mistake of showing enthusiasm at the manager's offer to show us "everything." Thus we stand for an hour on a freezing floor while one by one the entire stock is brought galloping down the corridors, half-dragging the grooms onto the central ring. But just as my love of horses is fading away, we move out at last to the sleighs.

The pines rise to a hundred feet around a ten-acre field. The snow is perhaps a foot deep; the air never gets warmed by the lungs. There stand three sleighs, one drawn by a pair of Arabs with long eyelashes—their eyes longingly darting toward their drivers, who now and then raise a palm as though to promise action soon—another with three horses, and the largest drawn by five.

There is a board to sit on and a narrower board in front for the driver. The smell of oats, hay, manure is like the smell of life because somehow it means warmth. In my heavy New York overcoat, which here leaks air like burlap, I am maneuvered into an ankle-length coat of embroidered felt three-quarters of an inch thick. The sleeves are wide enough to accommodate opposite fists; the broad collar, turned up, reaches above my head. In a moment the heat of my body returns from the felt wall to warm me, and as we start off the dreaded wind simply passes overhead as though I were in a heated cabin.

Troikas fly, borne aloft not only by the speed of the horses but by their joy. How those Arabs show off! And how the driver fights them. He has six reins flowing out of his fingers and drives with his feet on the dashboard, stretched out almost flat to pull those reins with all his weight. Just as in the books the pines flash by, the steam clouds up from the horses' rumps. The pounding of the hoofs on the snow soothes the mind. At the end, Inge Morath's trigger finger stands up crookedly, frozen useless. Ice hangs from the broad mustaches of the drivers, and I understand for the first time the protective utility of facial hair.

In a sort of conference room we must have a parting vodka. The manager and his staff pour it out in tumblerfuls. Their pride is all over them, their country fitness, an overwhelming masculine rootedness in what they are doing. We drink. Surprisingly the vodka goes down easily, as though the fuel it supplies merely makes up for what the cold has used up. We thank them for their trouble, and as with so many Russians facing the foreigner, they cannot help showing their pleasure at being hosts, a modest sort of satisfaction that you have found something interesting, a great dignity filled with pride and simple joy.

After a week or two one feels the need to know what is happening in the world outside, news from home especially. But unlike the main hotels in the capitals of Europe, where the Paris *Herald Tribune* at least is available, the newsstands in the Moscow hotels only carry foreign Communist Party papers. (Since the invasion of Czechoslovakia even most of the Western Communist papers have vanished.) The fear this implies is a shock at first. There is also something humorous about it; what better proof of the decadence of capitalism than *Le Soir*, *The Daily Sketch*, and their like in America? Or is it that even the worst tabloid, appealing to the universal thirst for the sensational, makes life appear so interesting in Europe?

It has often been said that Russia in many ways is now having its nineteenth century. And it is impossible to think of anything peculiarly Russian which is at the same time of this era. There have been serious composers of the first rank, a great many instrumentalists and classical ballet dancers, and there are certainly many good writers, but whether it be a new sound in music, a break-out in dance, an invention in prose that might illuminate the consciousness of the *nowness* of this time, it is not there. Even her high achievements seem so classic-bound.

Can it be that all feeling in Russia is historic, that there is really no strain of modernity in these people? It cannot be, not when one recalls Mayakovsky, the really astonishing theatrical work of Meyerhold and Vakhtangov and Tairov, who thrust a metaphoric theater into the place of the old realistic one thirty years before the West borrowed their methods, mostly without realizing where they originated. Life, Chekhov said, lies heavy on the Russian. But surely not this heavy. And in fact, painters exist who will not do monumental recelebrations of acceptable themes but strive to deliver up a vision of the life they feel. They cannot show publicly, however, and so the physicists let them hang their work in a physics building where a certain in-public crowds the unadvertised exhibitions.

Resolving again and again to forswear comparisons, I find it impossible nevertheless not to note the difference in mood between Russian and Western cities. Granted that in the West the line between art and crassest commercialism has almost vanished, that in the work of many writers sexuality has supplanted man's fate, that so much is a mere chasing after fashion and aimed at a lucrative market—concede the worst, but one fact remains. It is interesting, and it changes constantly. The streets of London, Paris, New York, Milan are in motion with people going somewhere. In Moscow they are all on their way home.

What can be so frightening about modern paintings that they must be kept in the basement of the Tretyakov Gallery, from which the public is barred? Man and the world are still commanded to look as they did in 1875, and at the same time the leaders who make and enforce these rules are perfectly at home with the shapes of their spaceships, with space-time concepts. And it is known that they receive *their* London *Times* and *New York Times* every morning.

No one can know why, as under Khrushchev, there have been periods of liberalization when a certain degree of doubt, protest, or modernism is allowed to appear in literature. Party leaders do not hold press conferences explaining such things. Surely no sudden flush of love for literature is involved, nor even a wish, for the sake of prestige, to begin to match the variety of the West's art. There can be only one explanation and it is that, in a system grown so complicated, total centralization and conformity do not work. The liberalization of the arts has to be understood as an integral part of the release, comparatively speaking, of people in industry to exercise a greater degree of individual decision and initiative. The relative decentralization of decision-making in industry came about because the system lacks feedback. A decision in Moscow affects millions of people all the way down to the meanest village, but if it is a wrong decision, if its results are contradictory or even ridiculous, there is no free press to relay the news back to Moscow. The press's function is that of a house organ—it propagates the original decision, justifying it, rallying support for it, and denying any evidence that it cannot work. So some kind of leeway must be given the press if only for the sake of efficiency. Similarly with writers. Literature is a kind of feedback, the rawest kind of evidence of what sharp and imaginative observers are making of the reality around them. If writers too must merely celebrate the system, where will the voices be found to correct what needs to be corrected? There is more self-congratulation in a Russian newspaper than in a campaign brochure of an American presidential candidate.

But this is not merely a technical question connected with increasing production. It is equally a spiritual one if only because, whatever the rationalizations, there is finally no legal recourse for an ideological offender. Put another way, if you tell the truth at the wrong time you can be punished, you can lose your right to appear in print with that truth and any others you may have at hand. The closest thing we have to such a situation is in the corporation, which requires loyalty first and always, its top executives reserving to themselves the decision as to what is helpful criticism and what serves the competitor or the corporation's enemies.

The nagging question, therefore, is whether these periodic expansions of liberty can really turn the trick, or whether an opposition must finally be legalized if only to keep the party itself from atrophying. But the very thought is a horror not to be borne by the fundamental theory of Leninism itself.

And having said all this, it is necessary to add that there is a profound grandeur here, like a sphinx, a human construct of devotion and endurance, forced obedience and genuine communal conscience, that is finally with all its failings a sublime attempt to create a condition of self-respect in a culture that was always cursed with master-slave relationships. All the slogan-jobbery, the obvious propaganda manipulations of Christlike values, the fake humanism, and the pervasive presence of the secret police—all of it still leaves intact the spectacle of the Russian person himself, the Russian who is still child of the spirit, still so openly aspiring to the transcendent condition, still so swept by an imperishable need for a goodness, a communal brotherhood that is not of this world. Whatever epithets Russia has ever deserved, "trivial" is not one of them.

In Tashkent once Inge Morath was taking pictures in a park. Along its border was a line of perhaps fifty framed color photographs, three feet by five feet high, of party and trade-union leaders. The subjects wore uniformly serious, official expressions, the kind of look the mayor of Ashtabula, Ohio, would have used for his photograph in 1912. Under the gloomy shade of the trees this immovable line of tinted faces, slightly faded by the weather, watched the twisting lanes and benches of the park, which at nine-thirty of a Sunday morning were nearly empty excepting for a few old men here and there reading their newspapers in the quietness. Down the path on which we stood I saw a drunk weaving his way toward us.

He wore unironed cotton trousers and a threadbare shirt. His hair was uncombed and wet as though he had just stuck his head under a pump. Seeing the camera, he came to a weaving halt, raised his arm, and pointed for a silent moment at Inge, who turned to him and waited.

"In America," he said, "you don't like the colored people."

We waited again, for he had either misplaced the rest of his thought or was having trouble speaking at all. But he was only trying to control his lips, it turned out. "In America you don't like many people. Here we like people. We like all kinds of people in Russia. Truly, everybody in Russia is nice. Everybody!" And lowering his arm, he walked past us in deep thought. Inge turned back to the line of official photographs and went on taking her pictures.

But there are, of course, other kinds of drunks with different revelations of the social condition. A few miles out of Moscow there is Peredelkino, a writers' colony which Gorky inspired Stalin to build. The homes are large and rambling wooden villas set in trees, on lots of perhaps an acre each. In one of them lived Boris Pasternak, the Russian poet and novelist whose last book brought down on him the fury of the Writers' Union, Sholokhov's curse (he called him a "pig"), and at his death a funeral which was attended by young writers as well as some older ones whose presence was intended both as an act of respect for the much-loved poet and a protest against his treatment by the authorities. Because Pasternak lived here and is buried in the nearby graveyard, Peredelkino is off limits to foreigners lest some of them set off a pilgrimage that could be embarrassing.

But there is no knowing exactly what "off limits" means in Russia. I have ridden in official chauffeur-driven limousines accompanied by government translators to prearranged, officially sponsored gatherings, only to be stopped by motorcycle police who made the chauffeur accompany them into a little hut beside the road, where, presumably, he had to prove his mission. We could drive with Galia, Yevtushenko's wife, in her little Moskvich to Peredelkino with no one paying any notice at all.

At the outskirts of Moscow, stopping at an empty crossing for a traffic light, Galia remembered an incident at this spot. Some years before, when Yevtushenko was enjoying his first high fame, he was driving with her and in their usual style they were having a discussion at the top of their lungs. Galia is a beautiful woman who would be hard to fool; Yevtushenko is a handsome man trying to eat life. She has seen everything once and is now watching it as though for the second time; he is newborn each morning. He went through the red light.

The siren behind them forced Yevtushenko to the curb. The militia man stopped his motocycle and, like traffic cops everywhere, took his time dismounting and walking toward them. In the interval Yevtushenko turned to Galia and said, "All right, now you'll see how famous I am. Watch this. An ordinary cop and see what he does."

The cop came to the window and said, "You went through that light."

"I was talking to my wife."

"Your license."

Yevtushenko, savoring his coming joy, handed his license through the window and watched for the recognition on the cop's face.

"*You* are Yevtushenko?"

"That's right. I am Yevtushenko."

The cop looked at him with astonishment, but strangely the stern reprimand had not left his face. "And you don't know the regulations? You drive like this, *you*—and your brother the Chief of the Moscow Militia?" A Yevtushenko, it now appeared, was indeed the head of the police. The poet took the summons in unaccustomed silence.

Galia, her foot pressing the accelerator to the floor, laughed until tears came to her eyes. "But what's the use? He'll never drive sanely," she said, and the tiny engine screamed like the straightforward passions inside this woman. We arrived at the parklike colony and Valentin Katayev's house.

Katayev is nearing seventy, like Ehrenburg a survivor, one of those whom Stalin did not destroy. If fire is cold to one's hand it is easy to look down at such men; if not, one can only feel a sense of wonder at man's durability. He has traveled in Europe and America, is a sophisticated, soft-spoken, witty man with large sad eyes and a full head of hair not yet gray. There is nothing parochial, nothing narrowly national about his attitudes, and one of his last books, *The Holy Well*, is a lyrical quest for a lost love in which, as though by-the-way, the mysterious immortality of the idea of human freedom is a leitmotif. Sitting with him on his sunny glassed-in porch, one realizes that at seventy he has lived through the whole agony of the last half-century of Russian history and must have known terrors that reached into the bone, must have wrung rationalizations out of his own mind to justify what he saw, must have died many times. And indeed, he wrote novels which had passages of idolatry for Stalin, passages which he could excise without disturbing the rest of the text, and did so after the Death. Since then he has come forward as a strong defender of writers and liberty and has become a sort of bridge between the younger men and the regime. Perhaps it is my own narrowness, but with all the men of this generation I feel constrained, as though there are large painful areas our conversation must avoid, and yet for all I know he is ready to talk about anything.

We walked with Galia and Inge a half-mile from his house to a glade he wanted us to see. A few acres of grass around a small pond surrounded by great old trees. Near the pond was a concrete basin covered with moss, and an iron faucet dripping water into it, and nearby a small bench. In this country silence he gestured toward the trees, the dark pond, the sky. "It is a microcosm of the whole world here. This pond is all ponds, those trees are all trees, the water from the tap is all the flowing water in Greece, Italy, America. One needn't move from here. Nothing else is necessary." Galia did not answer him, nor did we. In the silence one had to wonder what the two were communicating with one another, for she seemed filled with his message as she stared at the water. This, after all, was not a microcosm of the world;

there were no powerful men here, for one, no struggle to prevail, no blind ignorance, no petty hatreds. Was it that after all the struggle there turned out to be only a few, very simple, and very old unideological truths?

It was too cool to stay still very long, and we walked down a country road and came to a plowed field muddy from the recent rains. The furrows arced upward to a wide clearing in the distance, surrounded by trees, where the graveyard lay. Inge wanted to photograph Pasternak's monument. Neither Galia nor Katayev raised the point, but it seemed from their constrained agreement to lead us there that a visit to this grave was forbidden or at least frowned upon from on high. Now a man suddenly approached along the road, or rather a voice, an unbroken recitative delivered to the air in a mechanical dead-level monotone, the words spitting out loudly, with no emphasis and no pause.

As the stranger approached he seemed drunk, excepting that he was walking straight, very fast and very urgently. Seeing him, Katayev instantly turned away and walked quickly, all of us following, but the man caught up and rudely grasped Katayev's arm. He was dressed in blue woolen trousers and a heavy woolen shirt and wore a four-inch-wide leather belt strapped around his middle, army style. A kind of anxiety in his voice, an urgent message in his ruddy, tight face, and the breathless monotonous want of music in his speech suggested some commands he must be giving, but Katayev was not even attempting to pay attention, simply working at freeing his arm from the man's strong grip and shaking his head denying something. Finally he freed himself and we walked away, and the man remained behind, calling more loudly and anxiously to us as the distance between us grew.

"What is he saying?" I asked.

"It is nothing, nothing," Katayev replied, and a kind of ill look was in his face now.

We walked on in silence. It was strange to feel fear in this countryside, it was strange to live in a place where a grave could be dangerous. After a moment Galia said, "He is mad, that's all."

I was surprised—although now that she said it, it seemed obvious. But why was Katayev so depressed, perhaps even sickened?

He seemed to sense my question. "He is quoting Pushkin. It is a *folie de poésie*, a literary schizophrenia."

"Do you know him?"

"He lives somewhere nearby. I see him walking around occasionally."

"He always does this?"

"Always. He goes about like that, roaring out those beautiful lines. Whole pages, page after page. It's terrible, it's a ghastly thing."

"Is he a poet?"

"I don't know. I don't know what he is," Katayev said, and went silent, flinging the subject away like some painful memento.

The headstone is a shaft some four feet high, widening toward the top, where a profile of Pasternak is carved in low relief, so low that it will probably vanish into the stone in not too many years. On the grave tributes had been laid—flowers, stalks of wheat, a few apples which were in different stages of decay—as though a rather steady trickle of visitors came here through the weeks, months, and years. The grave, like all the others, is surrounded by an iron fence shoulder-high, and we entered through a hinged gate and stood there looking at the ground. The only sound was that of the camera shutter. Katayev now did nothing to hurry our visit, but when I indicated I had stayed long enough he moved out through the gate at once, with what I thought was relief.

We would take a different path back to Galia's car, which she had parked somewhere nearby so that we would not have to walk all the way back to Katayev's house. In a few minutes we crossed a railroad track and came on a nineteenth-century railroad depot, a steep-roofed, wooden building with fretwork eaves, the kind Tolstoy might have died in. I rarely take pictures, although on occasion I carry our 8-millimeter home movie camera just in case. As we walked past the little depot I noticed two drunks leaning against the building and talking. They had such striking Russian faces, and in this isolation and under these very old trees they seemed such everlasting types that I whispered to Inge that she was missing a great shot. Surprisingly she shook her head decisively and continued walking on. I said I would shoot a few feet with the movie camera. "Don't do it," she said firmly. She was raised in Nazi Germany and a sixth sense guides her judgment on these things, but her political caution seemed absurd to me here. When we had gone on about thirty yards, I took out the camera, turned, and using the zoom lens started shooting the two disputants. In the camera sight I saw one of them noticing me. Now he broke away from his companion and was walking toward me. I put the camera away. Galia, who had been walking in front of us, sensed through the back of her head that there was trouble. She turned and saw the approaching man and immediately walked back to meet him, barring his way to me with her body.

"I want that film," the man said. He was sobering up fast, and held out his hand to me.

Galia pressed his hand down and talked rapidly. Their voices were rising. I told Galia I would give him the film, that it didn't mean that much to me. She would not hear of it. I offered again, and she insisted it was silly and unnecessary, and went on arguing with the man. Now she flicked her hand toward me and said we must go on and she would catch up. And I saw that for her there was some grand issue here which she would not allow to pass. I was her guest, for the moment; I had no intention of maligning Russia with this innocent piece of film; she was damned if she would submit to censorship—for the man had begun by saying, "I am an official; I am a soldier of the Red Army."

Katayev, Inge, and I walked on, leaving Galia with the man. Their voices sounded more reasonable now, and glancing back I saw that he was behaving stubbornly—staring down at the path to listen to her but at least no longer threatening. We walked until they were out of sight. I looked to Katayev for what to do next. He was obviously intending to continue walking. Whether it was anger or fear in his silent face I could not tell, but in either case he seemed to know more or less what it was necessary to do. "Should we wait here?" I asked him.

"No, she'll catch up with us."

We walked on for a moment. "Why don't I just give him the film?" I asked. "I don't want to get her into trouble. It's foolish."

"Do as she says."

We walked on. There was evil in the air, it was impossible to go on conversing. Every instinct was being ground down, pulverized with each yard lengthening out between us and Galia all alone back there. Katayev was pale now. A wind had come up, cold and damp, and the sky was darkening for the night. We recrossed the tracks—not at a planked crossing but over the ties themselves, like escapees evading detection. Time enough had passed to know my own feelings and to guess Katayev's, but I also mistrusted my own knowledge of this country and I dared not do something that would bring serious difficulties to these people. We came to a paved road and halted. Galia would be coming from the right in her car.

We stood at the roadside, watching the road. An engine sound came from around the bend. We watched, but it was a truck. Then silence again. It is hard to stand in silence on a country road with a man one hardly knows. I no longer remember what subject I brought up to fill the wait, but we managed to exchange a few words to disguise this absurdity; but nothing could help and the silence returned between us, and a deepening sense of humiliation. This man was in his seventies, a widely respected writer, and here he was with his guest on a country road with night coming on, waiting for Authority somewhere to release him from his apprehension.

Galia was laughing when she pulled up before us. Laughing and shaking her head at the childishness of it all, and we were all talking at once as we drove back to Katayev's house, like children who had begun to think they were lost in a forest and now had accidentally found the path out. A victory had been won, it seemed—but over nothing.

In Katayev's dining room his wife was waiting with a meal on the table. There is a depth of feeling in the way a Russian woman sets food before a stranger. Katayev could drink only water, not wine. As I recall, he talked at great length about his times in Paris, a city with which he is passionately in love.

IV

If an invading army should ever fling itself upon the shores of California and sweep toward Washington, its air force smashing every standing structure, its strategy baffling the defense and overwhelming whole American armies in one massive onslaught which would soon put the capital itself in danger, it is not likely that an American President would have the time or inclination to send out a special team to load onto trucks the contents of William Faulkner's Oxford, Mississippi, house in order to safeguard for the nation the great writer's effects. Nor would this be regarded as a lapse of duty, or the destruction of the property a depredation particularly more meaningful than all the other destruction.

Yet at the height of the chaos during the Nazi invasion, Stalin's men removed Tolstoy's hat and stick, his coats, boots, and chairs, his books, dishes, and desk—the contents of the rambling old wooden home at Yasnaya Polyana —and secreted them all until peace had come. The Germans stormed in and, indeed, barracked soldiers in the house, and leaving it on their retreat accidentally burned part of it down. In a gesture of contempt for the old man's bones, which lay nearby under the tall birch and fir trees, they surrounded his grave with their own dead in this glade where long ago he had sat with his grandchildren, offering a kopek to the one who would *not* think of a white bear.

This tenderness toward the memory of a great artist is ironical in a country which, under all its regimes, never hesitated to censor art and not infrequently exiled recalcitrant artists or even killed them. There is surely an element of travesty in dialectical materialists turning the great mystic's home into a shrine. But there is a certain logic in it too. As I have indicated, the roots of Socialist Realism, the official Soviet credo of all art, are in Yasnaya Polyana.

Socialist Realism, an aesthetic yardstick which frequently is made of rubber and sometimes of oak hard enough to crack any skull, is not a uniquely

Russian invention. It demands that a work not merely report life as the writer has seen it, which is mere naturalism and inevitably an escape from the higher truth. That higher truth is made of several parts, chief of which is the superiority of socialism as a civilization, and its inevitable ultimate perfection in Russia and its victory in the world. Thus, a Soviet character who is shiftless, dishonest, with alcoholic tendencies, let us say, and constantly on the lookout for a dishonest ruble, cannot at the same time be a fervent supporter, let alone an official, of the Soviet state. It is not that such people do not exist in all countries and in Russia too, but that they are not typical in Russia. The word *typical* is crucial, and it means that negative characteristics, intellectual confusion or depravity, self-interestedness, careerism, and so on, cannot be ascribed to a socially desirable or socially important person. The higher truth, in short, requires that good be done by good people and evil by evil people. More, typicality means that every art work is at bottom a metaphor of society, however subtly social forces may be disguised in it, so that the outcome or impression of the work must be supportive of socialism as it is practiced in Russia. For a work to conclude differently would have to be a distortion of the truth and therefore bad art. As for art in or about capitalist countries, its metaphor must equal the decadence or anti-human qualities of capitalism; otherwise it is untrue and bad art. Furthermore, the texture of a work, its style and language, must be available to almost everyone. Since art always teaches, whether the artist means to or not, it must teach in favor of humanity, and the cause of humanity is socialism.

Tolstoy spent periods of his life writing essays and tracts to prove that it was depraved self-indulgence rather than art which merely provided sensuous pleasure, enjoyment, or time-wasting amusement. Art must be of use, mainly as a means of opening the eyes of men to the god within them, their inborn goodness. State, church, and other institutions exist only to keep man in ignorance of his real inner self, the more easily to send him into wars for the gain of his masters, or to pit him against his fellow man, the better to seduce him with material wealth and privilege, which kill his soul and enslave him to selfishness.

As a man, Tolstoy tried, sometimes desperately, to shed his own noble privileges—his alienation, one might say—and if his wife had not made it impossible would have published his works without royalty. He stood with the people, down to the lowliest, and art for its own sake was nothing short of sin.

Tolstoy is published in immense editions in Russia. If his religious dedication is an inconvenience in Soviet eyes, it is a small one—he merely reflected truthfully his own historic moment, and his shortcomings are the shortcomings of history; had he lived on into the Socialist era he would no doubt have been a Soviet writer. He is a Soviet writer now, in any case, since some of his writings are still unpublished.

The problem can be seen when it is admitted that in the months and years when Tolstoy was obsessed with teaching and writing educative tracts, his production of fiction fell away. And when his mind was swept with a story and characters and the sensuous spectacle of human beings acting as human beings do, his output of tracts ceased. The fact remains, however, that a Tolstoy shorn of his moral passions would be a mere storyteller.

But it takes a genius of this high order successfully to fuse his moral and social vision with profound compassion for man and his artistic conscience. In lesser hands, the command to teach through art results in neither good teaching nor good art but an art of facsimiles. There is nothing wrong with Socialist Realism as an aesthetic theory, only provided that the artist is indeed a Socialist Realist. If he is not, the theory, especially when it is administered as law and enforced by censorship, is a crippling thing. In a word, Tolstoy would never have stood for it.

The relics of great artists are always misleading. What detritus they leave behind we stare at for meanings and hints of their inner lives when in fact they hardly noticed such things at all. What posterity sees as a life-purpose and design for living, to the artist was makeshift, chaos more often than not. Tolstoy's house is a rambling wooden thing like thousands of other country houses the nobility lived in, but probably none of them with such an austere, workable—one might call it a modern—air. Here is the dining-room table where he tried to shut his ears to his wife's business plans, keep his eyes from his daughters' fancy clothes and the—to him—petty ambitions they signified, and listened like a child to sycophantic compliments of manipulating disciples. Like Pushkin's house, it stands apart from its age in its simplicity. One tries to resist the romance of such a place but in its silence, surrounded by snow and forest, Tolstoy's presence makes itself felt if only because the absence of any splendor speaks of a man at work here, and work in this house meant several masterpieces scrawled onto paper by the gigantic man on the second floor.

Still, he was a fool, like every other man, and caught in a domestic world he had made and could not recognize as his own, striving to slip out of his skin to enter the arena with God, whom he wanted to ask certain questions. Upstairs is his working area, a plain desk and a chair as low as a child's, which brought his eyes close to his paper and obviated the need for spectacles —for he was vain. It is all comfortable but somehow bare, like a prize ring, without the trifles, gewgaws, encumbrances so dear to Victorians. In his stories and novels he is a vast magnifying glass collecting the emanating rays of the Russian people, focusing them to a burning point which scorches their name on the ageless rock. Today it is Socialist Realism they justify by his work, tomorrow it will be something else. He saw life whole and one walks through his hallways believing that one day it will be permitted to see life whole again; somewhere high in the ranks of the powerful there must surely be men who know that for Leo Tolstoy there could be no mediator between a man and truth, not the church and surely not the state, socialist or capitalist, and among the Russian tourists who in summer come by the thousands on buses to walk in hushed silence past the bed he died on and the hat that shaded his eyes from the blazing sun, there are surely some who have received from his work that awareness of an awful, remorseless conscience which tests every work and every boast of man. One leaves Yasnaya Polyana with no worry that Tolstoy has been captured or used for purposes not his own; it is good that they keep his name alive. He is far more powerful than the nets of any program, political or aesthetic, just as the truth is in its survival despite everything. In a strange way it even seems that their strategic idolatry is an expression of their final, unadmitted wish to keep alive the rule by which they may be corrected one day, for the purpose of literature can only be to tell the truth.

But it is not only Tolstoy, of course, who is enshrined in Russia. Lenin's mummy and Stalin's (until he was placed underground before the Kremlin wall), a wax figure of gigantic Peter the Great, merely seem like weightier elaborations of the feeling which has embedded color photographs of the ordinary dead in headstones everywhere. The Russian icon is not merely an art form; the unwillingness to give up the body is reminiscent of ancient Egypt. And it may help explain their love of realistic painting and writing and, among other things, their actors' doting on noses.

After the performance of *A View from the Bridge*, backstage talking to the actors, I kept looking around for the actor who had played Eddie, the hero of the play, and since he was not present I referred to his performance several times, saying, "The man who played Eddie . . ." until I noticed a certain shifting, an embarrassment among the actors, and it was pointed out finally that their Eddie was standing next to me. He was totally unrecognizable. For the characterization on stage he had built up a different nose.

At the Sovremennik (Contemporary) Theater the troupe is very young, but several characters in Efremov's dazzling production of Schwartz's *The Emperor's Clothes* are aged men. The oldest, a prime minister who trembles with senility, turned out to be a twenty-four-year-old actor, and on another night I watched him for two hours in a different role and never realized it was the same fellow. It is all in the nose, and the changes are not always gross. A widening of the bridge, a slight tilting of the tip, a new flare for the nostrils and the actor is catapulted into another age bracket and a new personality. Gogol, of course, was fascinated with noses, and physical description in

Russian literature has traditionally been of great importance. People, whatever their psychological nature may be, are first of all bodies, and this fascination with the way people look is, I think, the foundation for the vividness of so much Russian acting.

A great deal has been made in the past twenty years of the staleness of Russian theater. Certainly it has kept out Ionesco, Beckett, the whole absurdist mode. But there is very little in the West that can match the vitality of the best Russian productions. Directors like Efremov and Lubimov would be of first importance anywhere. Their productions are highly finished and complete, yet imaginative and sometimes wild. Their actors are mostly young, full of enthusiasm and curiosity, and far better trained than the majority of Americans.

Even in plays with little distinction or novelty of form there is always some startling acting. *Uncle's Dream*, a dramatization of a Dostoevsky story, is a case in point. A great nobleman is passing through a provincial Russian town and his carriage breaks down. He must spend the night. The ladies of the best families vie with one another for the honor of sheltering him. The nobleman is unmarried, so naturally the mothers of eligible daughters are desperate to receive him. These are "the best people," and the nobleman is the incarnation of state authority and aristocratic distinction. The ladies meet in the living room of an important matron to decide who among them will have the honor. They have all agreed, however, not to invite Madame X (I have forgotten the character's name), who is universally regarded as a viper and a pest. Ten or twelve of them in satin and embossed velour dresses move about the stage, plotting, sweeping from couch to piano to the bust of Byron to the French doors opening on the garden, like a flock of excited geese, their words lengthening out into a kind of whining, half-sung chorale which nevertheless remains this side of reality. Comic as it is, it is somehow hair-raising. They sit down at last, sipping the drink of the cultivated—chocolate. In comes Madame X, who has gotten wind of this meeting to which she was denied admission.

Serafina Birman, the actress, as I later found out, was the age of the character—in her mid-seventies. She enters. The company falls silent in a hush of horror. The offended socialite stands center stage, surveying her betrayers. She begins to take them apart one by one, their private bad habits drawn upon their foreheads by her mocking, searing voice. For three minutes she continues without pause or mercy. Then four, then five, then six, then seven. Her breath begins to come hard, but she will not relent. She is unsteady on her feet now and takes a faltering step to the side as though about to collapse, but she goes right on. Suddenly—she goes down on one knee. Her brown satin gown, a veritable drapery, catches on her heel, her hair is falling into her eyes, but her bitterness flows on. She is losing her breath altogether, it seems, she is shaking in every bone, and she lies down on one side, propped up by her elbow, her free arm extended as she points from hated face to hated face. However collapsed, she never loses her nobility, her stertorian frightfulness, her righteous wrathfulness. She continues gasping out her curses, and now she lowers her free hand to the floor, turns over on her stomach, and points at the hostess, the arch culprit. "And as for you—I spit in your chocolate!" With which she sits upright, gets her feet under herself, and stands, swaying with exhaustion and a certain profound pleasure, and staggers out of the house. It is beyond acting, it is apocalypse, and backstage later I found for the first time in my life that I was pleased that someone had been given the Order of Lenin. She has been acting for over fifty years.

The physicalness of Russian acting, its mortal quality, was apparent also in what can only be called the disembodying of the nobleman. He appears at first as a caricature of an upper-class dandy. Obviously made-up to look young enough to attract women, he can barely move about in his patent-leather shoes, the lace pouring out from under his sleeves, the high stiff collar manacling his neck. Alone, finally, in a bedroom with his valet, he is being undressed for the night. The wide-chested jacket is removed, revealing a skinny torso; his gloves off show veined and aged hands. His fine head of hair goes into the wig box leaving him bald, his teeth go into a jar and his lips pucker up, and finally one eye comes out and there he sits, the mummy of the ruling class still chattering on about his possibilities as a lover. Of course the idea is not new, but the detail is so deftly etched that it still frightens and illusions the onlooker, who can only marvel at it.

No one who goes to the theater in Russia can fail to be struck by the audience. It is not bored and it is not uncritical, but it is passionately open to what it has come to see. Outside on the street there are always dozens of people pleading with each arrival for an extra seat. Young people make up the majority of the audiences, and particularly if the production offers something new and contemporary there is almost an atmosphere of adoration in the house, and open gratitude to the author, the actors, the director. It is as though there were still a sort of community in this country, for the feeling transcends mere admiration for professionals doing their work well. It is as though art were a communal utterance, a kind of speech which everyone present is delivering together.

The earthiness, the bodiliness, so to speak, of Russian acting even extends into its stylizations. Yuri Lubimov's production of *Ten Days That Shook the World* in his Taganka Theater is a sort of visualization of the atmosphere of the Revolution, rather than a play. From time to time a white screen is lowered over the whole stage, and, lit from behind, it shows the silhouettes of the actors, the people of the city caught up in the chaos. The detail of each silhouette instantly conveys not only that one is a prostitute, another a bourgeois, another a worker, another an old querulous gentleman, but somehow their attitudes toward the Revolution, and the impression comes from body postures, particularly of gestures, the way a head is held or a finger points. And as the light is moved back and more distant from the actor, his silhouette grows on the screen, so that at the end the figures of the new Red Army men, the defenders of the Revolution, move like giants as tall as the proscenium, dominating the whole theater.

Much of this production is sheer choreography and neither better nor worse than its counterparts elsewhere, but there is always some explosive conception which instantly speaks of this particular Russian genius for physicalizing. A young man is being held before a firing squad. He is let go to face his death. The rifles rise to sight him. There is no explosion of bullets, but the young man rises onto his toes, then comes down on his heels. Then he rises again, a little higher this time, and comes down harder. Now he jumps up a few inches off the floor and comes down; then he jumps up about a foot off the floor and comes down; now he is springing, higher and higher, his hands behind his back, until he is flying upward in a movement of both escape and pride, of death's agony and life's unbelievable end, until one imagines he will succeed in simply flying upward and away—and then he comes down and crumples to the earth, and no sound is heard.

It is wordless and physical, the diametric opposite of the poets' avant-garde theater which Yevtushenko and Voznesensky, among others, are attempting to create. Neither is primarily a dramatist but, as in most countries now, the theater has attracted poets as a public forum where contact with wide audiences can make poetry stretch itself toward its classic applicability to public discourse. By the accident of their appearance as spokesmen for the youth their names are usually coupled, but their talents and traditions are not at all the same.

It is impossible for a foreigner really to appraise Yevtushenko's "Bratsk Station" or "The Triangular Pear" by Voznesensky because they both depend almost totally on language. One can, however, speak of two different kinds of feeling that are quite apparent and distinctive in each. Voznesensky's is a first-person work, a series of stylized scenes allowing actors to speak broken-up sections of his poems as individual speeches. It is rather a staged recitative than a dialogue, but the power of his verse over the audience is unmistakable. The near-surrealism of the staging is sophisticated and charming, but it would probably seem rather tame in some far-out Western theaters. Immersed as one inevitably is in mass theater in Russia, which is basically realistic theater, this performance reminds one that there is an "in" culture and an "out," a split in the sensibilities of the country. "The Triangular Pear" celebrates personal emotions and an individual's singular reaction to his time rather than any group or public destiny and if it has a moral purpose it is to raise up to view the response of one individual to the world he has found. Its beauty of language apart, perhaps it is this quality of individuation which attracts the young to it and to Voznesensky's verse. He pretends to speak for no one but himself, his own nature. It is also probable that this is what unnerves the authorities about him.

"Bratsk Station" is of another order, a sort of cantata embracing the sacrifices, the endurance, the heroism of the Russian people as well as hints of the injustices they suffered in the gigantic construction of modern Russia. With a cast of perhaps thirty young actors, using Egyptian slavery as a symbol of Stalinism, the work strives toward a Whitmanesque celebration of the people's victory over their history, their betrayers, and those who would enslave them. The work opens with a movie projected over the entire back of the stage, showing on grainy 1920 film stock a long line of workers with arms linked around each other's waists, rhythmically tramping their immense felt boots on soft concrete into the forms of the Bratsk Dam. Moving en masse from side to side over the cement, they perform a kind of massive Hora of brute human power driving a twentieth-century structure into the ancient Russian earth. The film appears again at the end, after we have seen how this very discipline and faith was taken advantage of by slave-driving betrayers, but this time it is interrupted by a rush onstage of a line of well-dressed, shiny-faced young couples who break into an arm-linked dance to the same rhythm as the old Bratsk workers use in the film—now, however, with a rock musical accompaniment which joins both generations together in the present. The new young people throw off an air of free and joyous energy which inevitably seems to taunt any who would do to them what was done to their fathers. And the one refrain of "Bratsk Station" is, indeed, "Russians never will be slaves."

Seeing these plays it is difficult to understand why they should have met with such opposition from the party if it were not still torn between rather primitive Stalinist and liberative factions. There surely seems to be no split in the audience's enthusiasm, nor does there appear to be any sense of scandal or exposé in the audience reception. That Russians never will be slaves is hardly a revolutionary slogan and a regime which permits such sentiments on its official stage would merely seem to be feeling rather secure about its passage through a dark time. But the fact is that "Bratsk Station" went through many party-imposed revisions and line-changes. Only recently it was even taken out of production for a time and then allowed back again. It is all a little reminiscent of our afternoon with Katayev when we walked and talked in the countryside much as one would anywhere, and then suddenly there was fear—which never quite materialized in punishment but which might have.

Ultimately there is an absurdity about this alternation between repression and freedom, and beyond the absurdity a question as to whether the leadership is, or dares to be, in touch with the people at all. If the invasion of Czechoslovakia is any guide, it is not. Justifying the invasion on the need to rescue the Czech Communist Party from counterrevolutionaries, the Russian government was unable to find a single Czech Communist leader of any repute who would come forward as a representative of the rescued. The Russians found themselves forced to treat with the very leadership against whose betrayals of Communism they had come to save the country. This bespeaks either total cynicism or a hermetic, self-induced illusion of such proportions as to astound the foreigner—and doubtless many Russians too. (The problem came up in conversations with Czech intellectuals in Prague in March 1969. With Soviet soldiers occupying their city, they were under the gun, yet they were not entirely able to dismiss the possibility that the invasion was to some degree the result of self-delusion on the part of the Soviet party, a sign of its incapacity to recognize realities which its a priori theories denied existed. Russian officers and soldiers stopped people on the streets in the early days of the occupation, asking to be led to the "counterrevolutionaries," and were shocked by the hostility of the Czechs. Others believed they had landed in West Germany, because the people were so antagonistic, and as well because the shops were so full of gadgets unseen in Russia; the miniskirted girls and the general absence of fraternal sentiments helped this impression, too. The Czech intellectuals, however, filled with indignation and apprehension for their own futures, did not overlook the implicit naïveté, let alone the blind stupidity, of Russian pronouncements on the invasion. One lesson they seemed to draw from the experience was that in their own country—and, it is to be hoped, one day in the Soviet Union too—a legalized opposition must be allowed; not only to hedge power with law and law with the free-spoken opinions of the people, but also to prevent the party from atrophying. And finally—although they are neighbors, fellow Slavs, and fellow Communists—these Czechs find the atmosphere of religiosity surrounding the Soviet government as odd as it is to us. They did not, for example, admire the all but total silence of Russian intellectuals toward the fate of Czechoslovakia, but at the same time agreed when I said that for Russians to stand openly against their government is akin to heresy, with all its implications of guilt and sinfulness. Indeed, one could almost say that the rock on which Soviet moral presumptions broke apart in Czechoslovakia was that Czech socialism in its two liberalizing years had become anti-ritualistic, practical, and humane. In this view the purpose of the collective is the flowering of the individual; for the Soviets the collective is its own end and justification, the individual remaining a theoretically unaccounted-for, free-floating object whose real nature has never been fitted into the system.)

There is not supposed to be any anti-Semitism in the Soviet Union. It is all the more vehemently denied, especially as being part of state policy, because it was so blatantly a part of the Nazi ideology. A short time ago, however, a respected Soviet writer submitted for publication a series of memoirs of Russian writers of the twenties. The work was accepted with enthusiasm by the board of the publishing house, but, as always, there were a few editorial problems which needed talking about. One of the poets discussed in the work, a man who died in the early thirties, had been a Latvian German, and naturally had a German family name. His middle name, however—this, the editors felt, was an interesting variation of any German name they had ever heard of. In fact, they wondered aloud, it seemed to sound like a Jewish name.

The memoirist, a Russian of course, had never considered this at all. It was a name. He did not know if the middle name was Jewish, but if it was—did this represent a problem?

Not at all, the editors replied. But why must it be included? Why not call the man by his first and last names and simply leave out the middle name? The poems themselves were thoroughly Russian; why throw some sort of pall of misunderstanding over them? The poet's middle name was dropped.

Another Soviet writer—who shall also be nameless—wrote the story of the Bible for children. His rendition was also enthusiastically read by his editors. But, again, there were certain problems of a minor sort which required a conference, and one afternoon the author and his editors sat down to iron them out.

First of all, said the editors, there was this question of God. As we all know, God is a mythological construction, and in any strict sense mentioning God is really unnecessary.

But, replied the author, in the Bible . . .

Secondly, the editors went on, there is the whole business of "the Jewish People" cropping up again and again in your work, which is otherwise quite admirable. Why is that necessary?

Well, replied the author, the Bible, you see, is . . .

Why not simply call them "the People"? After all, it comes to the same thing, and in fact it generalizes and enhances the significance of the whole story. Call them "the People." And there is one final question.

The author waited for the final question.

It is the title. "The Story of the Bible" is not a very exact title.

What would you suggest? the author asked.

How about, "Myths of the People"?

And that was that.

V

Turning these pages of pictures one inevitably senses a certain gravity, a special sort of weight in Russian images. To me anyway there is a depth of sadness and at the same time a longing, an aspiration in what one sees there. Perhaps above all there is the sense of contradiction and paradox reaching down to the roots of Russia so that the longer one contemplates people and scenes there, the more convinced one becomes of a pervading imminence rather than a substantial extant factuality. If only because everything published is screened, if only because no two hundred and twenty million people can be quite so unanimous, one is finally sure of only one thing—that one does not know, and that maybe no one knows, what is going on below.

One night at a banquet, Khrushchev after a few vodkas turned to an American businessman of my acquaintance, a man he particularly liked, and asked him how many people he employed.

About four hundred, the businessman said.

Tell me, Khrushchev said, how do you get them to do any work?

The American answered: That happens to be one of our biggest problems too, motivating people to turn out the work. We pay them better and better each year, they get more and more vacation time and fringe benefits, but there is very little sense of responsibility toward the work itself. How, he asked Khrushchev, do you get your people to work?

Khrushchev then raised his glass in a toast to peace and friendly competition between both countries.

For fifty years experts have been saying that the Soviet system doesn't work, that it is on the verge of collapse under the bureaucratic load. Nevertheless, Russian stuff is flying around over our heads in outer space, and on the ground they have built what must be called an awesome civilization.

However, I cannot help feeling as I look at these pictures a certain muteness within them, and I do not think it is due to my own relative ignorance of the country. Old Russia hands finally admit the same thing—no one knows with any certainty what the Russia of today is *saying*.

It is hard enough to know this of a country with parliamentary government and free newspapers; to this moment you takes your choice as to whether the Nixon victory alongside the relatively low Wallace score plus the Republican failure to elect Congressmen represents a swing to the Right or the Left or perhaps sheer mental confusion. What does the present English government express about England, or the French about the people of France? More and more it seems as though the ideological make-up of a regime is rather an obfuscation than the expression of ideals or viewpoints. Western governments now are not so much compromises as chambers at the end of a *cul de sac*.

Perhaps it is simply that we are accustomed to the ways in which Western society fails to work, while the Russian failures are exotic and strange and always point to fatal, fundamental contradictions in the system itself. Soviet unfreedom, one sometimes feels, must ultimately lead to some kind of profound change, and there are days when the whole thing seems fated to explode. But perhaps it will only lead to more efficiency and a steadily rising standard of living. It seems to have done so in East Germany, the most rigorously Stalinized country anywhere.

The United States—if open resistance to authority is any guide—is the freest country in the world now. Yet there is no convincing reason why the prevailing moral turmoil will not ultimately lead to the kind of spiritual exhaustion which calls up and lends justification to a new authoritarianism.

If the problem is how to voluntarize human labor, how to arrange a world in which men contribute what they may to society and themselves rather than be driven by state discipline or hunger and deprivation, no society can claim victory. Indeed, we are universally losing ground.

If the problem is how to eliminate poverty and real deprivation, I would rather be a poor man in England, for one, than in the United States. I am not sure I would not be better off in the Soviet Union if I were poor, for that matter.

So when you speak of freedom you have to ask yourself who you are and what freedom you need. The poor man's freedom consists of not being poor any longer; for the middle class freedom consists of being necessary, at best, and at worst of being undisturbed in its quest of enjoyment and pointlessness. Which is your freedom?

These are the questions which lie underfoot like pebbles wherever one walks in Russia. In so many fields the corn grows in wavy rows, some plants much smaller than others. The fertilizer has not been spread evenly. Is it that they do not know how to spread fertilizer evenly? Or is it a muted expression of some peasant's contempt? Are these undulating rows crying out against a regimentation, a block-headed refusal to face the fact that a man will never tend a government-owned field the way he would his own? Or is there some other solution, some secret in the heart that neither social nor private ownership knows?

They have managed to pollute the largest lake in the world, Baikal, which was also the most undisturbed and perfect ecological arena left in Russia. One had thought only profit-seeking corporations did such things, but it was the Soviet paper pulp engineers. On a plane once to California an American oil engineer, a Stevenson liberal, told me that he was sure that with a few atomic explosions inside the Rocky Mountains he could release underground water sufficient to irrigate the entire American Western desert. But what about radiation, I asked? He was not interested in radiation, it was not his field. He was itching to make the desert bloom—or maybe he just wanted to blow up the Rocky Mountains.

One kind of freedom is surely the right to resist evil, but in a technological society is it really necessary? And if unused long enough does the idea itself atrophy and die? A dinner at the home of a very high official of a provincial capital presents a case in point.

His apartment was not mass-produced. A slab of polished black stone formed the fireplace wall, the well-laid parquet floors shone, a piece of modern sculpture stood in a spotlighted niche, there was an air of modernity, however vaguely out of date, about the place. A servant brought heaps and mounds of food, his wife was pleasingly fat, his young son spoiled by his constant embraces and melting, idolizing looks, his daughter's untroubled gaze like those one used to see around the dinner tables in our wealthier suburbs before America began to stink in the nostrils of the affluent young. He himself was a bit overweight, nearing sixty now, a novelist who had ceased writing since taking on his duties as union head ten years ago, but a good writer, everyone said, and humane. Now, instead of writing, he is a success; he must attend functions, fly on short notice to important conferences in Moscow, encourage young writers with literary lectures and reminiscences of his own struggles, advise and advise and advise. In all the *Gemütlichkeit* around the table one had to remind oneself that, at bottom, this warm fellow was and had to be the enforcer of the party's decisions on literature and no doubt on the fates of writers who had strayed from the path.

We drank and we talked and told stories and remembered books together and the war and we were civilized together. He wanted very much for the

Soviet Writers' Union to join International P.E.N., of which I was then president, so that writers from all over the world could forge a universal comradeship, or at least a common sense of values which might keep civilization from the wolves. By this time, we were close; any last armor of his official position had fallen away, and as happens with Russians at table with congenial company, they fall a little in love, and then a little more, until it becomes hard to imagine that issues could ever break this feeling they have for their guests.

And he admitted that he did not quite understand what difference Russian membership in P.E.N. would really make for them. For example, he said, what would our being members of P.E.N. have required of us in the Sinyavsky-Daniel business? What difference would it have made?

You would have had to protest, I said.

He looked at me. I looked at him. There was suddenly a sort of sweetness in his eyes. It was surprising. He was such a big man, and he had been a good writer once, and suddenly a foreigner he liked had said, "You, Yuri, you yourself would have had to endanger this apartment and your career, you would have had to come out from under what is weighing you down, and done what you know was right to do." In other words, the challenge had stirred what he was no longer sure he had any more, his soul. I had thought he might take offense, or slough off the challenge, but he understood it exactly, and he nodded. And then we talked of other things.

It is at precisely such moments that one realizes all over again why there has been such an ambivalence, so much uncertainty and hesitation, in the outside world as it confronts the spectacle of the Soviet official attitude toward humanist, democratic values. It would be so much simpler if a "Yuri" did simply take patriotic offense at such a challenge, if one saw no sign in his eye of this complete understanding of what one was talking about when one spoke of protesting injustice by the state. And that look is what for fifty years has raised the question—are they about to break through this unfreedom, are they perfectly aware of what must be done and merely awaiting the right or the possible moment to do it?

Or is it a dying look, the last flickering of a consciousness of fundamental human rights which actually are being engineered out of existence altogether? Which way are they going?

There are much-traveled roads with holes deep enough to swallow a car out of sight, some of them in the Caucasus where the edge of the road drops thousands of feet into the abyss. Is this a failure and decay, or the last day before the superhighway appears? On hundreds of two-and-a-half-ton trucks the right rear wheels wobble. On the other hand, my friend recently bought a new American car which he could not get out of low gear.

We were separated on the plane to Tashkent, Inge Morath sitting across the aisle from me beside two Mongolians. They were both over six feet tall and looked at her unsmilingly as she took her seat. The upper Mongolian eyelid has a curve at the outside corners, giving the face a fierce, frowning look. And with that built-in disapproval the man immediately next to her bent over to look into the book she opened as the plane took off. Her discomfort was evident as he continued to stare into her pages without any attempt to disguise what he was doing. His frown deepened until I was sure he was about to fly, for some reason, into a fury. Suddenly he jabbed his finger at a word, and said, "*Hoping?*" Inge looked at him. Yes, she said, that's right. His face burst into a smile. Out there where the wind never stops blowing, on some Mongolian plain, he had been studying English. He was an engineer Genghis Khan and happy as a clam as he went on jabbing his finger at words he recognized and which she, amazingly enough, could understand when he pronounced them.

In Tashkent they were rebuilding a vast part of the city after a disastrous earthquake, and cement dust clouded the air everywhere. In thirteen seconds two million square feet of living space had collapsed. Now, Uzbek, Tartar, Mongol, and Russian were working together to lay up the prefabricated concrete cubes which form apartment houses, and other cities were contributing, free of charge, all sorts of materials. Lumber from Leningrad, nails from Moscow, glass, bricks, flooring from the workers all over the Union. The place is a Klondike; a waiter shouts at us to make us get up from a cleanly set table and sit at a dirty one—evidently somebody important had made a reservation, or the waiter was just tired of cleaning a table again. We left angrily.

At night in the restaurant there are practically no women. The men—low-grade officials, foremen, technicians involved in the rebuilding—sit without much conversation, many of them obviously unacquainted with their table-mates, while a jazzband plays at them, trumpets at them, saxophones at them without gaiety, the right key, or the least charm. The playing is an assignment, joyless. The work goes on even in the silent, methodical ingestion of food. There is always a rubber plant.

And at the same time one knows that but for this sodden, plodding, grace-less motion of thick-necked builders, party guys, organizers, and despite the cement already cracking in the houses and the floors already starting to buckle, there would be here the ancient sewer of the East, the eye-flies, the bodies in the streets, and a few cultivated darlings at the top. Wait twenty years, is all one can hope. Life now has no story, it is only a condition. Going up or down, though?

The Opera House in Tashkent looked so inviting, and they were playing

Leila and Mezhdu, based on the national epic. We must go. Some difficulty in arranging tickets on such short notice. We arrive promptly at seven for a seven-thirty curtain, in order to see what the crowd looks like.

The building is some combination of Moorish, Spanish, City-Center-type architecture, but nevertheless very white and imposing, with wide-open concrete aprons around it and a nice flat stairway rising up from the street level. A strange quiet, however, as we pass beneath the outer archways, and in fact there is nobody in the lobby. Did we misunderstand the curtain time? It appears not, for the large lady usher takes our ticket and bids us follow her inside. Perhaps Uzbeks do not speak before the curtain goes up?

In the auditorium there is not one soul. Immaculately clean, the seat-arms polished, the carpet soft and well-vacuumed—but not a soul. We sit in the third row center. It is a vast house, with perhaps four thousand seats. Endless balconies, galleries, boxes. All empty.

Ten minutes pass like an hour and a half. Another couple comes down the aisle. Action! They are English. One can tell after a few minutes because they don't speak to one another but sit at polite attention quite as though the seats around them were full. Nothing whatever is odd, remarkable, wrong. If water started rising above their ankles they would not move or take note. One loves them, their truly *interested* attention as they stare at the empty orchestra pit. England will never die.

Movement behind us. Turning around I spy a customer. An Uzbek worker, he wears a cap sideways, a red bandanna around his neck, no shirt, his black wrinkled jacket and pants and shoes caked with white cement. He is alone, lounging in his seat, staring at the curtain up ahead. Things are moving. Soon we may have the ushers outnumbered and could force a performance.

A disturbance in the orchestra pit. A musician enters from under the stage. A man of sixty, his eyeglasses badly bent, he has no tie, wears a sweater. He sits and opens his violin case. Something wrong with the bridge. He adjusts it for ten minutes.

More action behind us. For some reason about eight people have entered the second balcony. Five or six are now spread out behind us in the orchestra, one man sits alone in a side box.

Two more musicians enter the pit. One of them tests his clarinet, the other reads a newspaper. How forlorn. Three or four more come into the pit now. They tune up, but only barely take any notice of one another. Perhaps they have been exiled here? One, for some reason, is wearing a tuxedo. Probably a recent arrival from Moscow, still unaccustomed to frontier mores.

The tuning-up is getting louder and is much better than nothing. Suddenly, as though on cue, they all stop, pack up their instruments, and walk out under the stage! Can it all be over?

Inge is now weeping with laughter, a certain hysteria having entered our relationship. Neither one of us can say anything that is not funny.

A small note of revolt—the audience begins to clap in unison. It is now a quarter past eight. The English couple remains fascinated by the curtain, takes no note of the demonstration. The clapping dies away. Begins all over again.

The house lights go down as the musicians hurry back in. A full orchestra, the members glance out over the gala audience. A kind of utter exhaustion emanates from the conductor, who makes a play at a rapid, sprightly entrance. Somebody up in the gallery claps once.

The curtain rises. An Arab-type chieftain sits before a cardboard tent surrounded by his court. He seems angry as he sings baritone. The others try to placate him. He is stubborn, refusing comfort. Moussorgsky weaves through Tchaikovsky through intermittent Rimsky-Korsakov. Ignorant of the story, one still knows that the chieftain's daughter must soon appear. She sure as hell does. Beautiful girl, but can't sing. Which is the hero? Two or three young bravos appear and one knows which is the hero because he is the shortest and stands at the center, and whenever he points at something he also takes a gliding step in the same direction, while the others only point without taking a step. Very gradually one's sympathy begins to go out to all of them knocking themselves out for the empty house. What dreams of glory they must have had once! It is terribly hard work, this opera. Queen Victoria would have adored the purity of its emotions, the sweep of the music. It is all Cultural. Somewhere in this city must be some guys and girls hiding in a cellar playing some stringed instrument and singing to each other without a committee. The public has vetoed this opera, is all one can say. It has definitely decided to risk everything and not come. There is something heartening and universal, finally. As the box-office man on Broadway once said to me, "There is no power on earth that can keep the public from staying home."

Intermission. The audience rises. The combined sound is like eleven chickens scratching in Madison Square Garden. We stroll idly, politely, toward the lobby. The English couple, still *interested*, appears a few yards away. I confide to Inge that we are not remaining for the second act, although there is no doubt the English couple will do their national duty. We stroll out the front door rather as though wanting a breath of the night air. We keep on strolling at a sort of trot. Glancing behind, we see the English couple also strolling, looking about at the nonexistent native audience, but disappearing nevertheless into the bowels of Tashkent. And yet—what's the opera situation on a weekday night in Duluth, Minnesota?

In ten years there will be forty million more Soviet citizens. Most now are under eighteen. The leadership is in its sixties.

In public places here and there are man-height posters listing the moral attributes of a good Soviet citizen. The emphasis is on cooperation, politeness, patriotism. If one did not know better it would seem the whole place is some gigantic post office and everyone its employee.

One never hears, "I don't know why we did that." It is always, "They . . ."

There is an old Samarkand and a new. The old is naturally more interesting but smells of sewage, which in fact does discharge into gutters alongside the dirt streets and alleyways. The old part is on the way to being torn down, however. Two synagogues stand side by side on one of these streets. A covey of aged and near-aged men sits in the little yard before them. They are eager to show me inside, where there is a sharp smell of new paint. The buildings are ancient and rickety, but immaculate. Much woodwork, painted sky-blue and trimmed with the same brown color one can see in old New York synagogues. It turns out to be a favorite Russian color, like earth perhaps. The interiors of old railroad depots in New England were painted the same color, a sort of international public brown, you might say.

The old men were proud of what obviously was their own renovation. They showed off old, cracked Talmuds, broken-backed prayer books, like treasures. Unfortunately, we had a translator, a young Russian student, whom the old men, I thought, did not quite trust. Things, they said, were not bad at all. I asked if any younger people attended the synagogue. Not many, in fact hardly any; the young are all too busy with other things.

They seemed astonished at the two visitors dropping down on them from outer space. Fascinated, in fact, but never asked a question excepting where we were from. I asked what was going to happen to Judaism once they were gone? One old man replied, "God will take care of that. He always has." I added, since he stopped at that, "And of course there is Israel." He nodded. By this time word had spread and there were two or three women and a dozen or so men standing and watching our attempts to communicate. Inge suggested in a whisper that I contribute to the poor box. But I was taught never to carry money into a synagogue. Nevertheless, as we were leaving, I put some rubles into the box. The onlookers remained interested, but expressionless. We left, having learned nothing.

After a time outside the big cities one begins to long for less determined-looking women. A few pass by now and then, but in the provinces most of the women's faces seem tougher, more work-hardened, more proletarian. It is like a cost of production. They are working, working hard. It is a country being built stone by stone, board by board. Bridget Bishop was arrested on suspicion of witchcraft in Salem in 1692 because she took to wearing a red ribbon around her middle. They hanged her. What we have come to call femininity is a correlation of a surplus; where there is scarcity, individuality is evil as it implies a tendency to look in the mirror in mourning for one's life, instead of getting out there and digging with the others. And you can't help respecting their attitude, whatever its cost to them.

Everyone says there is little crime, but I have never seen so many ways of locking things up. Perhaps that is the reason.

In the cool of the Samarkand night, hundreds of young standing around in the park square for the jazz concert. Many young soldiers. No loud shouts or dashing about, but everyone well behaved, clean, short haircuts. The girls hanging together in clusters, pretending it was only the music that brought them. The tension in the eyes of the fellows on the make, yet hardly looking right or left, gazing at the band up front. Most seem poorly dressed by any standard, some pathetically so, but with a certain innocence and gravity even, almost a sense of responsibility since they are in a public place, are *citizens*, and ought to behave. Russians are country people.

Suddenly one is aware of an emanation from within the crowd. Two sharpies are moving over to a group of girls who make to ignore them. They wear sunglasses, these two, and pointy shoes, and one of them has three rings on his left hand, and they know the music is square but they try to drive it along by snapping their fingers and heavily nodding their heads to the beat. Slouching with the peaked eyebrows of sophisticates, they survey the provincial scene, turning, turning endlessly, searching among the faces for the break, the sign, the thing. But the girls are remorseless, never glance at them and their coiffed long hair and hidden eyes. Now the two move away, snapping their fingers, their heads turning, turning, as they seek the border and all the great things happening somewhere in the world. The cement dust gleams in the spotlights hung on poles over the eager band. One of the musicians, the only one who makes it with the music, is a Red Army private. He stands now and blows his clarinet. Whatever restlessness and polite attention there was in the crowd his music draws to a hard point of real joy. Suddenly I am happy that there is no mistaking what is good, anywhere. A biological aesthetic that transcends the borders, the moralities, the bloody mistakes of the boobs who run the world everywhere.

I could be wrong, but the farther from Moscow one gets, the longer it takes for the sugar cubes to melt in the tea. Near the borders you have to stab at them with a spoon, and finally chew them.

A woman poet takes us through the Novodyevichy Cemetery near the Kremlin. It is an elite cemetery for the families of the leaders and there are many elaborately carved tombstones, many large photographs of the deceased, some in color. Her grandparents were among the early revolutionaries, and her grandmother fed her porridge saying, "This spoon is for Papa Lenin, this spoon is for Papa Stalin, this spoon is for . . ." so she can't stand any of them, she says. But she looks at the various graves with the familiarity of one who knows the occupants: generals, commissars, heroes. To her they are individuals—fools, seers, liars, or decent souls. And one slowly realizes that she is like a daughter of one of the First Families, even an aristocrat, and indeed she has all the inner sadness, the disillusion, and the impeccable standards of the nobility which can neither bear the grossness and posturing of the current "elite" nor turn their backs on their people. "Poetry that is not great is not good. Emotions that do not subject a person to their dangers are counterfeit emotions. Truths half-told are half-lies," she says suddenly.

We arrive before an extraordinarily simple marble shaft, chest-high, with a well-modeled head of a woman on top. It alone is not crowded by other graves. A few yards before it is a stone bench only wide enough for one person. It stands near a door in the brick wall surrounding the cemetery. It is the grave of Stalin's wife who shot herself. He would come here at night and sit contemplating the grave. The poet, strangely, does not mock this fact. She stares at the stone seat in silence. For two years during one of his purges she lived hidden in a cellar. She was not quite twelve then. Both parents were shot.

There is an almost universal conviction that all hotel rooms are tapped, as well as many apartments. Visitors sometimes arrive with paper and pencil, communicating by writing while they carry on banter directed toward the bug, or at home play loud Beethoven passages while discussing anything of importance. The odd thing is that after a while one gets used to it oneself. Transistorized cartridge tape recordings are also good masking devices. One sits down to discuss some ordinary matter, and the host turns on a loud rock-and-roll number in his lap. Pretty soon, though, a sort of surrealistic mood develops, especially if the conversation is a sad one, or if both parties to it lapse into silent thought for a few moments while hillbilly music squeals on. When the recorder is turned off it is time to eat, or speak of happy or inconsequential things. But should the serious mood return again, on goes the tape recorder and the rock-and-roll. Ultimately it is an incredibly pleasurable thing simply to go to bed and think freely to oneself. Maybe this is why so many Russians seem so deep, and despite their gregariousness so solitary —perforce, they have done so much communing with themselves.

It may also be part of the explanation for the special importance of literature to them. So much that is ordinarily unsayable is given by the nuances of good writing, by its capacity to imply far more than its syntax, transmitting by definition a climactic social application. Thus the pressures on the writer and artist are compounded, and the contradictions too. Nowhere else are writers so close to being worshiped by their readers, nowhere does a regime go to such extremes to honor or hound them. The paradox is built into the writing craft itself, for on one hand nobody, not even the commissar, denies that writing to be any good must be personal, must be an individual's own thought and style. On the other, by expressing his individuality the writer takes hold of a certain power, a power which he must not use beyond the point where the regime feels comfortable with his use of it. Thus, periodically he must be humbled. It is as though there were an arena where the talented may venture at risk, and the seer or prophet at the risk of his life. The importance of literature stems, finally, from the penalties hanging over the practice of it. Thus a writer is always a step away from dread heroism and is worshiped like a sacrifice. After all, writing is almost the only act one cannot in Russia commit anonymously; even the great physicists and inventors are rarely credited by name, so that whatever power might accrue to individual scientists is waylaid. But a novel or play or poem cannot very well come into the world by itself, or as the result of a committee's resolution, and the power of authorship is thus unique; only the leaders can be so well known, and therefore in danger of such idolatry—or such humiliation, should conditions change.

Perhaps it is also why they so detest frivolous or fragmentary or self-indulgent writing. It is like telling bad jokes at a funeral or in a church. In a very real sense the national fate is in the writer's hands, the immortal fire of the race. And so the wrath is terrible when he appears to have some secret allegiance to foreign ideas, and it is very probable that that anger is not confined to the bureaucracy alone. Whatever the repressions it may use to perpetuate itself, there must surely be a deep strain of apathetic consent in the people or they could not possibly continue.

One could, and one ought to go even further, and face the fact that there is such a thing as working-class taste, or more precisely, an unalienated taste of whatever class. So many attempts have been made in England, America, and France, for example, to establish trade-union theater movements and thus to break through the ring of bourgeois audiences and middle-class prejudices and tastes. They have never come to anything. It seems as though people who are deeply immersed in the production process, people who spend their lives trying to make things work, and have, so to speak, invested themselves in sustaining and elaborating the productive process, are not going to enjoy a spectacle which lacks materiality, reality, purpose, and logic of an everyday kind. Every machine process moves from less to more, from nothing to something, from the imminent to the accomplished. Conflicts of thought, abstract symbolizations, much of the arsenal of what is called modern art, lack point for these people because, while these qualities may *be* something, they do not apparently *do* anything either to move such people, to educate them, or to give them an idea about themselves. The Soviet hierarchy may well be basing itself upon the innate conservatism of all producers, and especially those who have no reason to be revolutionary. After all, the fame and impact of a Brecht was created with and among the alienated bourgeoisie and not among the working class. Finally, Solzhenitsyn, the one writer in Russia who is universally regarded as a classic, a genius, precisely fits the ultimate categories. He is a seer, an absolute truth-teller, and he writes simply, realistically, in a style untouched by the past fifty or even seventy-five years of literary experiment, a style which any literate worker, engineer, or schoolteacher can bite into and find nourishing. His latest books circulate in typewritten drafts, but they are not published. Yet he is known everywhere. He alone has had the audacity openly to call not for a relaxation of censorship but for its total abolition. He has entered the arena of the saints. And it needs to be added that there are not many writers anywhere in the world with this kind of insight, to say nothing of his courage, a courage which is not only expressed in the political implications of what he is saying, but in a style which dares be comprehensible to the alienated and the unalienated alike.

Our last night in Russia, inevitably, brought all the incipient chaos of feelings and unanswered questions to a head. Andrei Voznesensky and his wife, Zoya, good friends of Maya Plisetskaya, prima ballerina of the Bolshoi Ballet, had arranged for us to see her performance. Yevtushenko's wife, Galia, insisted we could not leave the country without seeing a certain painter's work in his apartment far from the center of town. Inge had meanwhile misplaced her passport. A Russian journalist who had broken his back in an Army plane he crashed in Siberia in an attempt to machine-gun a bear had insisted I take home a jar of special honey for my cold and would meet us anywhere. Appointments we had been postponing with three other people now had to be met. And through all these meetings and conversations and gift-giving Inge had to try to get through the telephone system to all the places we had been in the last twenty-four hours to try to locate her passport—a difficulty, when a lot of Russians do not answer their phones unless they have been notified ahead of time as to who is calling.

On top of it all there was a curious mood of uncertainty because a writer-friend of the Voznesenskys had just turned up; he had recently come under attack by the Writers' Union, which had gone so far as to publish an article against him in the press. The man some weeks before had gotten so apprehensive that he had gone off to a small town in Siberia to get away from the mutterings against him in Moscow. Now, just back, he was wondering if it had been wise to return. Then again, maybe he should issue some intransigent statement which might rally support for him; on the other hand, *would* others support him? Should he perhaps return again to Siberia? Should he go back to his own Moscow room? On the other hand, maybe he was overreacting altogether, and the whole business was unnerving him more than it should.

Meanwhile we were all moving into the immense crowd pressing into the Bolshoi Theater. To strange eyes it seemed as though the crowd had never before seen a ballet, the eagerness was so intense. We said good-by to the pale, uncertain writer at the stage entrance. He also knew Plisetskaya well and would love to go up to her dressing room and say hello with us, but maybe it was better he did not. We wound our way through the back corridors of the great theater; the public-address-system loudspeakers connected with the auditorium were alive with the powerful rumbling of people excitedly greeting each other as they took their seats out there. We climbed stairs, wound through other corridors, opened doors through sitting rooms, and the Bill of Rights seemed unutterably precious then, the sheer ignobility of hounding the man we had left in the street was a choking, enraging thing. Nothing, no progress could be worth the fear in that writer's face.

A gentleman in frock coat led us into a sitting room to wait until Plisetskaya had dressed. The walls were red velour, the Louis Something furniture covered with white sheeting as though waiting to be unveiled on some occasion of state, the mirror frames gilt, deeply carved—the very flower of the great age of the cataclysmic Czars. Here too the sound of the auditorium could be heard through the speakers, like a sea waiting to be calmed by the holy power of this dancer dressing on the other side of the paneled door. We waited, talked of the decor and its playful silliness, which now, however, seemed so innocent and naïve. Perhaps a Czar had sat here, made to wait a few minutes by some primping ballerina, for it all smelled of Power and therein lay its impressiveness and fatuousness. The frock-coated gentleman, the impresario actually, passed through with a nod to Voznesensky sitting there in his pea jacket and sweater, and opened the paneled door, closing it behind him. In a moment the door opened again—she was ready now.

We filed into Plisetskaya's dressing room. A hall of mirrors. She kissed Andrei. Some time ago he had written one of his best poems about her. They were in league with a spirit that shone in their eyes. She bade us sit down. I had never seen a human being move like this. A racehorse, her muscles swathing the bones. The costume was deceptively casual and peasantlike; in fact, it was an athlete's, like a fighter's gloves, a runner's trunks, and she shifted the waistband of the skirt a quarter-inch as though that infinitesimal adjustment would in a few minutes release her from the pull of earth. She was working now as we talked, turning her feet, ever so slightly stretching her shoulders inside her skin, and the sound of the packed house flowed over her from the loudspeakers, the adoring and menacing sea-rumble of Moscow.

A separate balcony about thirty feet wide hangs over the orchestra of the Bolshoi, in it two high-backed thronelike chairs flanked by lower ones for the noble retainers, the great red drapes framing it all with immense loops and flowings of cloth. The Czar was not in either of the thrones. The stage is very brightly lighted, the faces of the audience await the magic. The curtain lumbers up and *Don Quixote* begins. As a non-fan of classical ballet I decided to sit back in our box just over the footlights and interest myself in the sociology of it all, but as soon as the Knight's soliloquy was over and the girls came on, sociology finished. Each seemed six feet tall, full-bodied, and light as air. What woman could dance more beautifully than these? And Plisetskaya materialized, her body arched forward, it seemed, and her legs and arms shot backward, like a speeding bow freed of the laws of physics. The audience seems to be under her feet, behind her back, over her head, watching every flicker of movement she makes as an infant watches its mother move.

The act is ending. The music stops. She turns to our box, and suddenly I remember that she will be dancing a special cadenza for us. She glances up and begins. The audience knows something unusual is on. A hum, a subdued roar of an oncoming cavalry shudders the house. Wild, noble, unbelievably concentrated inside herself and yet abandoned to a love of air and space, she greets all poets, and perhaps America, with a freed body.

The pleasure of the audience now is like a statement, and the seeming paradox of the Bolshoi is straightened out; there is a mood here different from that in any other place I saw in Russia: the archaism of the house and the classicism of the repertoire are really the forms in which people can simply face beauty, beauty without the measure of utility, cant, or rationalized social significance. Here you are Russian and here you are free, and all the rutted roads, the toilets that don't work, the moralizing posters, all progress and all decay are far, far away as this woman transcends the dialectic and the mortality of thought itself.

We cannot stay for the second act and in Plisetskaya's dressing room we are all, for some reason, kissing each other. And we are off in Galia's little car—from the Bolshoi, as it turns out to the Bronx, a housing project where her painter friend lives—but it is necessary first to accept the jar of honey from the bear-hunting ex-pilot at the stage door and then to drop Voznesensky at his apartment because he is tired and needs sleep. And where has the pale writer gone to spend the night?

On the way out to the project the passport is suddenly discovered on the floor of the car; how it got there nobody can figure out. The buildings of the project are still under construction. They surround a vast open area which will be a park and is now a playground for bulldozers. A stripe of color across the building fronts is somehow encouraging in the night, a sign of the will to go beyond mere shelter. Galia, efficient as ever, knocks on a door two flights up and is greeted by a bewildered man holding on to his pants and blinking sleep out of his eyes. We flee down and finally stand on the sidewalk resolving to call out the painter's name in hopes he will hear. Modern mass housing must finally cure alcoholism; no drunk could pick out his own building from all the others. At last Galia recalls a house number. There at the head of the stairs is indeed a man awake, the painter, smiling, happy to see us again—for on a previous trip Yevtushenko had taken us here to see him. Now there are improvements, for while his parents still share the apartment he has a permanent girl friend and an additional room. We sit at the bare table surrounded by his immense canvases, drink vodka and brandy, eat salami, olives, potatoes, herring, and bread, and look at his work. He cannot exhibit publicly, but this hardly bothers him any more because he has an underground clientele. His pictures are massive and cryptic explosions of various shades of red and black, strange bloated men move through them cloaked like black-gowned priests surrounded by perfectly edible melons which, however, bleed. He eats, he drinks, he has a quite decent place to live in and an adoring girl and good friends among the poets, the scientists, the intellectuals. Compared to the last time we saw him he seems to have cast off his cares about government disapproval, not because it is no longer serious to him but because he has, perhaps, made his peace with the life he must lead—he will paint what is inside his spirit, and enjoy his food and his girl, and tomorrow will be what tomorrow will be. The perfect idiocy of artistic repression was never so vivid as in that room and in the laughing face of that Russian painter who could hardly bear to waste time by going to sleep at night. His blasting energy is there even in the way he chomps his herring. There is a challenge in this nearly bare room, and a ghastly thought: in the West, where everything in art is allowed , the artists feel unneeded by society, supercargo. Here, the repression is a mark of art's importance, otherwise why would government bother policing it? In which setting is the artist closer to reality?

We fly out. What a relief, like finally getting out of a six-thousand-mile-wide country full of Irishmen. They are, you know, a lot like the Irish when the Irish are just a little bit blasted. You never know what's going to come out of them next. Below, the clouds are closing over the plain of dead armies, the white birches bare, womanlike trees with tender skins, shivering in the snow. Europe soon, and the neon signs brightening the avenue, blazing shop windows full of beautiful things again, plenty. Plenty . . . and the blacks and the students hoisting strange flags on the statues, the magazines announcing revolution in five-color photos, cities on fire beside the green golf course, more bombs dropping on one Vietnam than on the whole earth in World War II, stereophonic sound in the new U.S. cars. Somewhere in Moscow that writer is standing in a hallway, wondering if he dare go home, and the Uzbeks are rebuilding after the earthquake, Yevtushenko is floating down a Siberian river on a raft, Solzhenitsyn's books are passed around in typescript, and in Chicago soon Allen Ginsberg will be humming his "O-o-o-om-m-m-m" to the enraged and astounded cops. The plane's compass steadily hangs on the "W" and thank God. But which way is man? Anywhere?

Possibly we are over Vitebsk now, Smolensk, Minsk, the old invasion path paved with forty million pairs of eyes violently closed; now Poland and Treblinka, Auschwitz, Berlin—the spinning earth should have splashed the sky bloody red by now, but everything is still so innocently blue up here, the dunning of propellers reassures, as though such dutiful precision cannot have come from a species altogether wedded to death. And indeed there are two Chinese across the aisle studying some papers and perfectly at ease, despite the murder in the air between Moscow and Peking. Is there still, beneath the polemics and the threats, an unadmitted commerce of a human kind? Or is there truly no fresh wind in any corner of the sky to blow away the fumes of fear we all breathe now, this terror of each other that will finally murder us all?

As we circle Warsaw, trying for a glimpse through the fog-wetted windows, the cabin so silent and orderly, the thought, for some reason, comes of *The Seagull*. And Chekhov spitting blood in the loneliness of Yalta, and writing those minimal and yet ultimate lines for Nina, the betrayed, suffering girl— ". . . to endure. To be able to bear one's cross and have faith. I have faith. I'm not afraid of life." How terrible that seventy years later, seventy years of the most astonishing acquisition of knowledge in man's history, it is so very much harder to speak these lines without fatuousness on this planet.

Piatnitza, a Russian sleigh drawn by five horses.

The clouds are scurrying and spinning;
The moon, though hidden, throws her light
Upon the flying snow; the heavens
Are troubled, troubled like the night.
I drive across the naked country,
The bell rings ting-a-ling; in vain
I try to check my terror, viewing
The enormous, unfamiliar plain.

   —ALEXANDER PUSHKIN
     From "Evil Spirits" (1830),
     adapted by Babette Deutsch

Up, out as if for early mass—
When we prowled through wild Leningrad,
We were more breathless than the dead
And lower than the sun.

—ANNA AKHMATOVA
*From "Requiem," adapted by Robert Lowell
with Olga Carlisle*

Leningrad. *Opposite:* Cathedral of Saint Isaac of Kiev as seen from the old Astoria Hotel. *Overleaf:* Palace Square, photographed from the Winter Palace. In the center of the square is Alexander's Column, which was erected by Montferrand in 1834. It stands 158 feet high and is claimed to be the largest monolith of modern times. The immense square has played an important part in the revolutionary history of Leningrad. The Winter Palace was occupied by the Czars at the time of the October 1917 revolution, and Hitler planned to hold his victory parade here.

Pages 70–71: Under the blue-green walls of Leningrad's Winter Palace. Built by Rastrelli between 1754 and 1764 as a residence for the Czars, the palace, together with the adjacent Hermitage, now houses one of the greatest art collections in the world.

In the sculpture gallery of Leningrad's Hermitage: *Amor and Psyche* by
Antonio Canova (*above*) and wax effigy of Peter the Great (*opposite*).

Peter
    the First—
Sweater
    the First. . . .

Not Tsarist (from furs swaddling,
from steam bath's musical coddling)
    But coarse
                and pleasant,
                        like a peasant!

—ANDREI VOZNESENSKY
From "A Ballad of Work,"
translated by Herbert Marshall

Leningrad. *Opposite:* A woman shoveling snow on Khalturin Street (previously Million Street), which runs along part of the façade of the Winter Palace and the Hermitage, parallel to the Neva Quay. Early in 1917, the palace became the seat of the provisional Kerensky government, which in its turn was ousted by the victorious revolutionaries on October 25 of the same year. *Above:* Street in the old quarter, around Saint Isaac's Cathedral, where Nikolai Gogol lived.

Leningrad. *Opposite:* Stone bust of Nikolai Gogol in the Workers'
Garden (formerly Alexander's Garden) in front of the Admiralty. *Above:*
The Nevsky Prospect, the city's most famous thoroughfare, at Anichkov
Bridge. Gogol said of this street:

There is nothing finer . . . not in St. Petersburg at any rate;
for in St. Petersburg it is everything.

　　　　　　　　　　—NIKOLAI GOGOL
　　　　　　　　　　　From "Nevsky Prospect,"
　　　　　　　　　　　translated by David Magarshack

Overleaf: Leningrad. View of the Great Neva and part of Ostrovsky
Island, from Falconet's equestrian statue of Peter the Great.

Leningrad. *Opposite:* Class at the State Ballet School on Alexandrinsky Square. *Above:* Scene from a play about teenagers performed by teenagers for a public of similar age in the city's new theater for young people.

Overleaf: Three Leningrad faces. The poet Iosíp Brodsky, who, after being accused of "social parasitism" in 1964, was arrested and sentenced to five years' hard labor above the Arctic Circle. After two years, Brodsky was released, and he now lives and works again in his beloved Leningrad. Nikolai Akhimov, scene designer, director, and painter, who until his death in 1968 was one of the most talented, modern, and influential figures in the Leningrad theater; and Danil Granin, the novelist.

Opposite: Iosíp Brodsky, the poet. *Above:* Artist Nikolai Akhimov with grand-children. *Below:* Danil Granin, author of the best seller *Those Who Seek.*

Leningrad. View of the Neva, the Palace Quay, and the cupola of Saint Isaac's Cathedral, from the roof of the Fortress of Peter and Paul. The building of the fortress, ordered by Peter the Great, was supervised by Tresini from 1703 to 1710. After losing its military importance, the fortress was transformed into a jail for political offenders. Its first famous prisoner was the Czarevich Alexis, son of Peter the Great. Alexis had led a revolt and was, on his father's orders, tortured to death.

Leningrad. Inside the Fortress of Peter and Paul, the prison of the Trubetskoy Bastion. The photograph opposite shows the door to Cell 21, in which Maxim Gorky was imprisoned in 1905. In Cell 47 Alexander Ulyanov, Lenin's brother, was incarcerated before his execution at Shlisselburg. The passageway is reached through two dark rooms, a guard's room and the chancellery where prisoners received their chains.

Osip Mandelshtam wrote about persecution, and the following poem, "Stalin," is said to have caused his arrest in 1934:

We live. We are not sure our land is under us.
Ten feet away, no one hears us.

But wherever there's even a half-conversation,
we remember the Kremlin's mountaineer.

His thick fingers are fat as worms,
his words reliable as ten-pound weights.

His boot tops shine,
his cockroach mustache is laughing.

About him, the great, his thin-necked, drained advisors.
He plays with them. He is happy with half-men around him.

They make touching and funny animal sounds.
He alone talks Russian.

One after another, his sentences hit like horseshoes! He
pounds them out. He always hits the nail, the balls.

After each death, he is like a Georgian tribesman,
putting a raspberry in his mouth.

—OSIP MANDELSHTAM
Adapted by Robert Lowell with Olga Carlisle

Overleaf: Each of the seventy-two cells is separated from the passageway by an oak door with a spyhole through which prisoners were watched.

A walk through Dostoevsky's St. Petersburg (Leningrad). Fyodor Dostoevsky was born in Moscow, but—except for five years in exile in Omsk, Siberia, and four years abroad (in flight from accumulated debts)—he spent the greater part of his life in St. Petersburg. Dostoevsky was restless and frequently changed apartments, but he always remained in the same part of town. He preferred to live in corner buildings, near a church and in the neighborhood of the troubled and the poor, and would use these surroundings as settings for his novels.

In 1967 Andrei Dostoevsky, grandson and only surviving descendant of the writer, took the authors on a tour which retraced the steps of Rodion Raskolnikov, the hero of *Crime and Punishment*. We met him at the entrance to No. 7 Pergevalsky Street, where both Dostoevsky and his hero Raskolnikov lived. Dostoevsky was very exact in his descriptions of sites and of the movements of his heroes. In *Crime and Punishment*, for instance, he wrote that Raskolnikov "had not far to go; he knew indeed how many steps it was from the gate of his lodging house: exactly seven hundred and thirty. He had counted them once when he had been lost in dreams. . . ."

Opposite: View from the window of Raskolnikov's lodgings, overlooking the courtyard. The window is next to the landlady's kitchen where Raskolnikov had intended to steal the ax and murder the aged woman pawnbroker.

Overleaf: Andrei Dostoevsky crossing Peace Square—called Market Square when *Crime and Punishment* was written. The novel says Raskolnikov "had often crossed that little street which turns at an angle leading from the Market Place to Sadovy Street. Of late he had often felt drawn to wander about the district when he felt depressed, that he might feel more so."

Above: Courtyard between Raskolnikov's lodgings and the pawnbroker's house.

Below: The hallway and entrance door to the flat of the pawnbroker, Alyona Ivanovna. Dostoevsky's

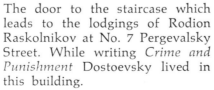

The door to the staircase which leads to the lodgings of Rodion Raskolnikov at No. 7 Pergevalsky Street. While writing *Crime and Punishment* Dostoevsky lived in this building.

Staircase leading to Raskolnikov's lodgings. "He met no one, not a soul, afterwards on the way to his room; the landlady's door was shut. When he was in his room, he flung himself on the sofa just as he was—he did not sleep, but sank into blank forgetfulness."

grandson is shown pausing in front of it, as did Raskolnikov, checking the ax and waiting to be let in by the old woman. "He was out of breath. For one instant the thought floated through his mind, 'Shall I go back?'"

She spends herself as, brightly dar-
    ing,
She flies, disdainful of those bars—
How like a lawless comet flaring
Among the calculable stars!

—ALEXANDER PUSHKIN
"Portrait,"
translated by
Babette Deutsch

Pushkin's Leningrad. Portrait of
Natalia Goncharova, whom Alexander Pushkin married in 1831. The
photograph was taken in the poet's
house, Moika 12, which is now
kept as a museum.

View of the Moika Canal from the apartment Pushkin lived in after his marriage. On February 10, 1837, he died here of wounds received during a duel with Baron Heckeren D'Anthès.

No, I'll not wholly die. My soul in the fond lyre
is to survive my dust and flee decay;
and I'll be famed while there remains alive
in the sublunar world at least one poet.

—ALEXANDER PUSHKIN
From Eugene Onegin
translated by Vladimir Nabokov

Monument to Pushkin in Tsarskoe Selo (now named Pushkin), where the poet entered the newly founded lyceum in 1811.

АЛЕКСАНДРУ СЕРГѢЕВИЧУ   Въ тѣ дни въ таинственны

Opposite: Writing desk in Pushkin's study, Leningrad. *Above:* Two girls in Pushkin on their way to school—the same school that the poet attended over 150 years ago. Behind them is one of the iron gates in the park of the Catherine Palace, summer residence of the Czars since Catherine II. *Overleaf:* Lake in the grounds of the Catherine Palace.

Pages 104–105: Staircase in Catherine Palace.

Inside Catherine Palace. Painting of the nude Czarina Elisabeth in the Chinese Salon.

Overleaf: Near Leningrad. The famous golden fountains at Petrodvorets, Peter the Great's "Russian Versailles" by the sea. The palace was built under Peter's orders by Leblond and Rastrelli between 1715 and 1750. Petrodvorets was the largest and most brilliant of the summer residences of the Czars. The palace and fountains were destroyed by the Germans in World War II but have been restored.

Mikhailovskoe. Pushkin was exiled by Czar Alexander I to this estate, which belonged to his great-grandfather Hannibal. Here the poet wrote many works, including *Boris Godunov,* parts of *Eugene Onegin,* and *Graf Hulin.*

I'm banished into myself
                    I'm Mikhailovskoe.
. . . . The
            River and I are the universe . . .

—ANDREI VOZNESENSKY
From "Triptych,"
translated by
Max Hayward

Left: C. C. Gechenko, authority on Pushkin and present conservator of the estate. *Below:* Bridge made of birchwood. *Opposite:* Onegin's bench. *Overleaf:* The lake.

Rostov Veliki, churches in the Kremlin. The town, which is about two hundred miles south of Leningrad, remained one of the capitals of old Russia until the Mongols destroyed it in 1474. Its Kremlin dates back to the seventeenth century, but its semi-military, semi-ecclesiastical function gave it a medieval appearance. Other churches inside the Kremlin are much older, such as the Cathedral of the Assumption, which dates back to 1164. The interiors are decorated with old frescoes painted by Moscow artists, including Dmitriev. In the center of the photograph is the tower with the bells that play the famous Rostov Chimes.

114

Rostov Veliki. Entrance to the White Palace, once the residence of arch-
bishops. *Opposite:* Street with arcades. In the background are the cupolas
of the Church of the Resurrection.

Overleaf: Novgorod the Great. This city, one of Russia's oldest, lies halfway between Leningrad and Moscow on the Volkhov River. Its name
symbolizes, more than that of any other Russian city, the mingling of
merchant wealth and ecclesiastic flowering which was an essential part
of the country's medieval pageantry.

Below: Novgorod. The Volkhov River and part of the Kremlin walls, which were first built of brick in 1302 and extended in 1490.

Opposite: Spire of an eleventh-century wooden church near Novgorod.

Overleaf: Novgorod. A peasant hut in the fields outside Saint George, one of Russia's oldest monasteries. The big cupolas at the right of the photograph belong to the twelfth-century church of Saint George, the last to be built by the great princes of Novgorod.

Opposite: Pereslavl-Zalesky. Local sculptures in wood of Jesus Christ and the head of Saint John the Baptist.

Then far and wide in anguish staring
My eyes, grown stiff with tears, will see
Down the broad river slowly faring,
Christ in a skiff approaching me. . . .

—ALEXANDER BLOK
From "When Mountain Ash,"
translated by Babette Deutsch

Overleaf: Pereslavl-Zalesky. Portraits of members of local families and a group of saints from churches of the region.

Novgorod. Soldiers sightseeing inside the Kremlin.

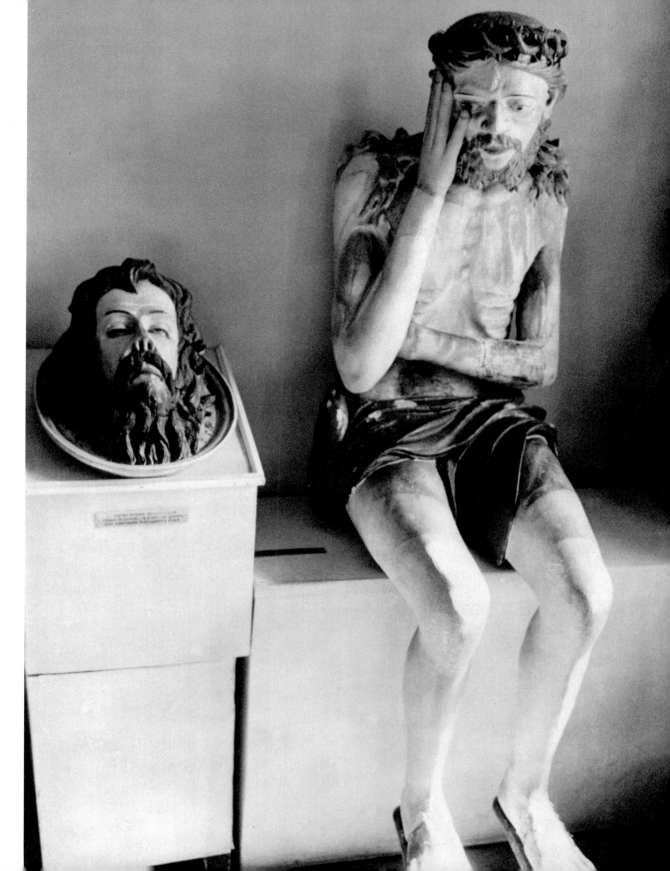

Zagorsk. *Above:* The famous Church of the Trinity, which contains the body of Saint Sergius. It was built in 1422 by the patriarch Nikon on the very spot where Sergius had built his original wooden church, and it still remains open for worship. *Opposite:* The main square inside Saint Sergius Monastery. In the background is the Cathedral of the Assumption, which dates from 1585, and the multicolored chapel which houses the tomb of Boris Godunov, the usurping Czar who died in 1605.

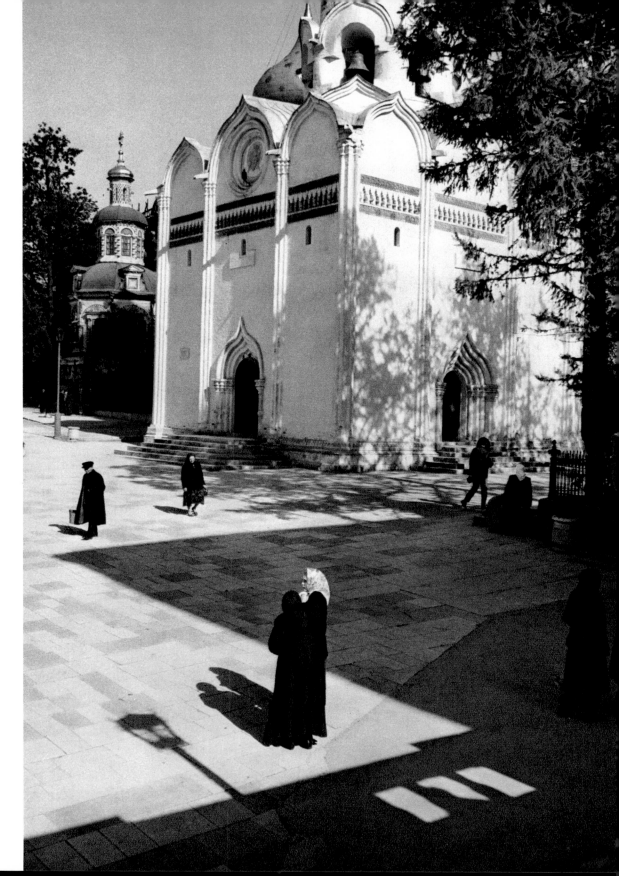

Above: Zagorsk. A monk working in the garden in front of the seventeenth-century refectory of Saint Sergius Monastery. The building is painted with multicolored lozenges which recall the "facets" of Moscow's old Kremlin wall. The interior has been converted into a church.

Opposite: Klin. Decorative statue along the Moscow-Leningrad road.

The town of Klin was made famous by Tchaikovsky, whose tomb (*above*) is in Leningrad's Tikhvin cemetery. *Top right:* The dressing table in the bedroom of Tchaikovsky's house in Klin. *Bottom right:* The composer's breakfast room. *Overleaf:* The terrace leading into the garden behind the gray wooden house in which Tchaikovsky lived until his death in 1893.

Kolomenskoe. This old estate of the Czars lies a little less than ten miles from Moscow. Here Ivan the Terrible had a palace, and it was here that Peter the Great spent part of his childhood, sheltered from the revolt of the *streltsy*. The view is from the terrace of the sixteenth-century Church of the Ascension, looking toward a fortified gate and the White Falcon Tower, where Czar Alexander raised hunting birds.

137

Two troika horses pulling at full gallop near Moscow.

Beneath the booming bells
Moscow is seething like a brew. . . .

To you,
Barbarians
Of all times!

Tsars, tyrants,
In egg-shaped crowns,
In robes of flaming fire,
And with the muzzles of your top hats!

——ANDREI VOZNESENSKY
From "Second Dedication,"
translated by George Reavy

Opposite: Moscow. Seventeenth-century Russian figures in full armor in the Kremlin's Palace of Arms Museum.

A corner of Moscow's Cathedral Square, the loveliest and most famous spot inside the complex of the Kremlin. At the left is the corner of the Facets Palace, built in 1491 by the Italians Marco Ruffo and Pietro Antonio Solario during the reign of Ivan the Terrible. The palace contained the Czar's reception and throne rooms, where the coronation ceremonies and rites consecrating patriarchs and metropolitans took place. In the center of the photograph is the small Church of the Deposition of the Dress of the Virgin. The wall behind the church, with its arched Renaissance windows, is the outer façade of the Czarina's golden apartment. To the right is the corner of the Cathedral of the Assumption, largest of the Kremlin churches.

Overleaf: Red Square on visiting days is filled with queues of people waiting to be admitted to the Lenin Mausoleum—the small, dark structure at the right in the background of the photograph. To the left is Moscow's biggest department store, the GUM, which replaces the old merchant stalls. Dominating the square is the magnificent sixteenth-century Cathedral of Saint Basil, built in the reign of Ivan the Terrible by the Russian architects Barma and Postnik to commemorate the conquest of Kazan.

141

Moscow, Cathedral Square. To the left is the entrance to the Cathedral of the Assumption. *Opposite:* The Czar Bell, in the Kremlin, weighing 465,000 pounds, is supposed to be the heaviest bell in the world. It was cast between 1733 and 1735, and soon afterward, during the great fire of 1737, it fell from its tower and became buried in the ground. It has now been restored as a monument. In the background is the Cathedral of the Annunciation.

Overleaf: Moscow in the early morning looking toward Red Square through the Art Nouveau grille of the Metropol Hotel dining room. The building in the center, the State History Museum, was designed in pseudo-Russian style by the English architect Sherwood in 1875. To the right is a corner of the Kremlin's fortified wall and the ramp.

Moscow. Inside the Tretyakov Gallery, an immense museum of Russian
art and painting, which houses some 50,000 paintings, icons, sculptures,
drawings, and other treasures. Particularly popular with Russian visitors
are the large canvases painted by members of the "historical school."

Moscow. Schoolgirls in
the Tretyakov Gallery.

Moscow. *Above:* Choosing mushrooms in the Central Market. *Opposite:*
Repair shop for watches and other "metallic objects."

I'll ask how much the woodsy mushrooms are,
And price the milk that shines in a cold jar,
The grapes, too, that a hawker has piled high,
The flowers a girl holds out to catch the eye;
I'll price the multicolored wealth of wares . . .
A pity that my pocket is quite bare. . . .

    ——ALEXEI MARKOV
     "At the Market,"
     translated by Babette Deutsch

Moscow. Street with immense apartment houses, typical of the modern city. *Opposite:* Inside the Novodyevichy Monastery, one of Moscow's landmarks. High brick walls, similar to those of the Kremlin, enclose gardens and churches with bulb-shaped domes, among which is the famous Trapeznaya, open to worshipers. Inside these walls Boris Godunov was elected Czar, and Sophia, sister of Peter the Great, sought refuge after she had handed over authority. Three hundred *streltsy* musketeers who had supported Sophia were hanged by her brother's orders under the windows of her cell, and the hand of her principal supporter, Prince Khovansky, was nailed to her door.

Overleaf: Tombs in Novodyevichy Cemetery, decorated with life-size busts of Arctic explorer Lieutenant Schmidt and Army General Zakharov.

Also in the Novodyevichy Cemetery (*opposite*) is the tomb of Stalin's wife, Nadezhda Alliluyeva Stalina, who shot herself. *Above:* Wall with urns containing the ashes of early revolutionaries. Since the beginning of the nineteenth century the cemetery has been a burial place for famous Russians, a Pantheon in a setting of trees and flowers. Among the writers buried here are Gogol, Chekhov, Alexei Tolstoy, Mayakovsky, Esenin, Ehrenburg; among the composers, Rubinstein, Scriabin, and Prokofiev.

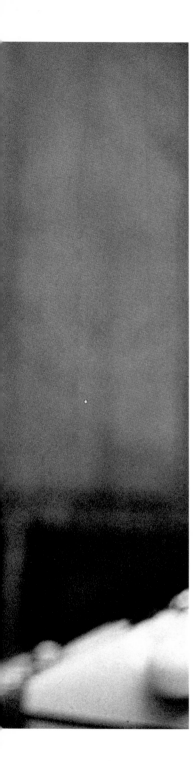

. . . .
I want
      the commissar of the times
            to lean
over my thought with an order.
I want
      my heart's ration of love
to be the extra one
            allotted to specialists.
I want
      the shop committee
            when my work is done
to secure my lips
         with a padlock.
I want
      the pen to be equal
         to the bayonet.
I want
      Stalin
         representing the Politburo
to report
      on the output of verse
as he does
      on the output
         of pig iron and steel;
"Out of workingmen's
      hovels
we've climbed
      to the top;
in the Union
    of Republics
        the appreciation of poetry
has surpassed
      the prewar level. . . ."

—VLADIMIR MAYAKOVSKY
From "Going Home,"
translated by Babette Deutsch

This poem was written in 1925 after the author's return from a trip to
the United States. The 14th Congress of the Communist Party was then
in session, and Stalin had presented the Political Report of the Central
Committee.

Madame Ekaterina Furtseva, Minister of Culture of the USSR, in her
office in Moscow. She was elected to her position in the post-Stalin era,
under Nikita Khrushchev.

Moscow. Backstage at the Akademichesky Theater in 1965, during the run of Dostoevsky's *The Uncle's Dream. Left to right:* Yuri Savadsky (a pupil of Stanislavsky who also worked with Vakhtangov), the director of the theater; Mme. Anismovoy-Wulf, stage director of the production; Mme. Serafina Birman, who played the unforgettable "floor" scene described in the text; Arthur Miller; S. G. Ranevskaya, who played the hostess; and K. K. Mikhailov, who acted the part of the elderly prince. *Opposite:* Maya Plisetskaya, the intelligent and beautiful Prima Ballerina Assoluta of the Bolshoi Ballet, chatting in her dressing room just before curtain time.

Overleaf: In a salon at the Bolshoi Theater, Arthur Miller with poet Andrei Voznesensky and his wife, the writer Zoya Boguslavskaya.

162

Moscow. Nadezhda Yacovlena Mandelshtam, widow of the poet Osip Mandelshtam, who died in 1938 on the way to a Siberian labor camp. Following his arrest he dedicated to his wife the following poem about their departure into exile:

You and I will sit for a while in the kitchen.
The white kerosene smells sweetly.

A sharp knife, a loaf of bread.
Why don't you pump the petroleum stove tight?

You can collect some strings,
And tie up our basket before sunrise,

Then we will escape to the railway station,
No one will find us.

—OSIP MANDELSHTAM
*Adapted by Robert Lowell
with Olga Carlisle*

Opposite: Drawing room in novelist Lev Kassil's house. *Left to right:* Madame Sobinov, widow of the tenor, under an early portrait of herself; her granddaughter; Lev Kassil; and his wife.

166

Moscow. In the study of Professor Mikhail Gerasimov, the anthropologist and sculptor. Gerasimov's specialty is to reconstruct the skulls and facial traits of historic figures from bones excavated from ancient tombs. Behind him is part of the impressive array of heads, including those of Mongol kings, which he has resurrected from the past.

Overleaf: In the atelier of Pavel Korin, who specializes in portraits, including religious figures of the past. The painter's vast studio is in an old wooden house which he saved from destruction. It stands in the back yard of one of Moscow's big new apartment buildings. The slightly larger than life size paintings surrounding Korin were waiting for the official stamp of approval (by a small committee) before being sent to New York for a show at the Hammer Gallery.

Moscow. Tea in the apartment of Mr. and Mrs. Ilya Ehrenburg. On the wall is one of the many Picassos. Talking to Arthur Miller (at left) is Natasha Stoliarova, Mr. Ehrenburg's secretary. *Opposite:* Konstantin Simonov, photographed at his country house in a writers' colony near Moscow. One of the Soviet Union's best-known prose writers and a hero of World War II, Simonov wrote a poem that most of his generation know by heart. The last of the four verses reads:

Just wait for me and I'll return,
. . .
And none but you and I will know
How I escaped the thrust of fate—
Simply because, better than all
The others, you know how to wait.

—KONSTANTIN SIMONOV
From "Just Wait for Me,"
translated by Babette Deutsch

172

Valentin Katayev in Peredelkino, the writers' colony about thirty-five miles from Moscow. Katayev has written verse, novels, screenplays, and comic-opera librettos. His play *The Squaring of the Circle* won him international fame. *Opposite:* The composer Aram Khachaturian, with his wife, pianist and composer Nina Makarova, in their Moscow flat.

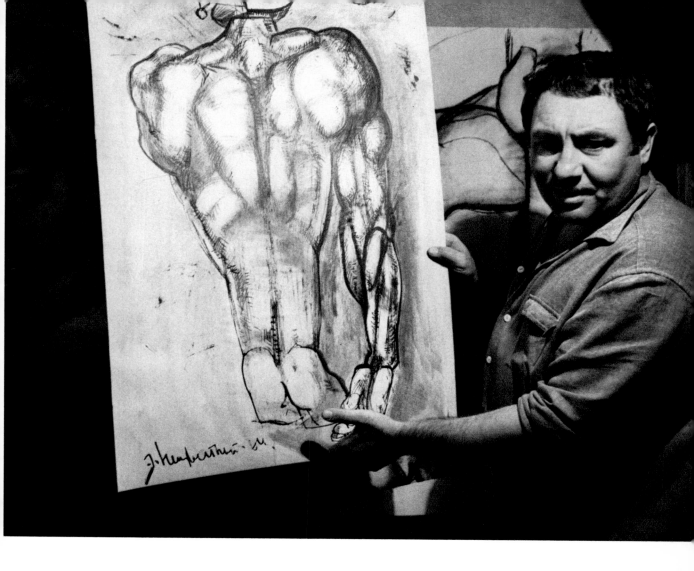

Ernst Neizvestny, one of the most influential artists in the USSR, in his Moscow studio. He was the prime target of Nikita Khrushchev's attack on modern art in December 1962, but he continued to work and has since been accepted on his own terms. When, at the meeting of the ideological commission of the Central Committee, Neizvestny was attacked for "unpatriotic formalist art," it is reported that the poet Yevtushenko defended him, saying, "Neizvestny came back from the war with his body crisscrossed with wounds. I hope he will live many more years and produce many more fine works of art." Khrushchev replied, "The saying goes, 'Only the grave corrects the hunchback.'" Yevtushenko then commented, "I hope we have outlived the time when the grave was used as a means of correction."

Oleg Efremov, movie and stage actor, director and head of Moscow's Sovremennik (Contemporary) Theater, photographed during a good-by party in the sleeper compartment of the Red Star Express, before the authors left for Leningrad. *Opposite:* Vasily Aksionov, the talented young writer whose novels deal with the life and problems of his generation. His short story "Halfway to the Moon" has been hailed as a masterpiece.

In the office of Oleg Efremov. Facing the camera is poet Evgeny Yevtushenko. *To his left:* Oleg Efremov, playwright Greenberg, with theater critics. The meeting had been called to discuss problems of the contemporary theater with Arthur Miller. On the wall is a portrait of Stanislavsky.

Opposite: Andrei Voznesensky, one of the finest Russian poets of his generation, received his first encouragement from Boris Pasternak. Much of his work has been translated into English, and during visits to Europe and the United States he has drawn vast audiences to his dramatic readings. *Above:* "Paris Without Rhyme," a scene from the dramatic adaptation of "The Triangular Pear" at the Taganka Theater, Moscow.

Overleaf: Scene from Director Lubimov's dramatization of John Reed's *Ten Days That Shook the World* at the Taganka Theater.

Evgeny Yevtushenko is probably the best-known of the Soviet's young poets. He has been in the avant garde of protesting Soviet youth who want to restore a sense of conscience and greater freedom in literary and public affairs. His poem "Zima Junction" made him famous in Russia, and he attracted attention abroad with his "Babi Yar." *Opposite:* His wife, Galia.

Scene from the Moscow production of
Yevtushenko's dramatic poem "Bratsk Station" in the Malaya Bronnaya Theater. A
few lines from it follow:

Pyramid,
        I am the daughter of Russia,
a country incomprehensible to you.
She was christened in childhood with a lash,
torn to pieces,
            scorched,
Her soul was trampled by the feet,
inflicting blow upon blow,
of Pechenegs,
            Varangians,
                    Tartars,
and our own people—
                much more terrible than
                the Tartars.

                —EVGENY YEVTUSHENKO
                Translated by Tina
                Tupikina-Glaessner,
                Geoffrey Dutton, and
                Igor Mezhakoff-
                Koriakin

Overleaf: Landscape south of Moscow.

I journeyed through Russia, with Galya beside me,
somewhere towards the sea, hurrying in a Moskvich
from all my sorrows. . . .
And, seemingly, with some kind of premeditation
hiding its essence till the last minute,
Russia prompted me suddenly, past Tula,
to turn in towards Yasnaya Polyana.
And now we entered the faintly breathing homestead,
children of the atomic age . . .
hurrying in our nylon raincoats,
benumbed, we suddenly stood still, hearts failing.
Descendants of peasant envoys seeking truth. . . .

> —EVGENY YEVTUSHENKO
> *From "I Journeyed Through Russia,"*
> *translated by Tina Tupikina-Glaessner,*
> *Geoffrey Dutton, and Igor Mezhakoff-*
> *Koriakin*

Yasnaya Polyana, the house in which Leo Tolstoy
lived from 1862 to 1910, lies about 160 miles
south of Moscow in the province of Tula. On
three occasions Tolstoy walked from here all the
way to Moscow. He inherited the immense estate
from his mother, Princess Volkonsky.

The ground-floor study in which Tolstoy wrote *Anna Karenina*. Sometimes he changed workrooms, taking his desk with him. *Opposite:* The dining room. At the table in the corner Tolstoy's family and friends used to gather to listen to him reading his latest work.

Tolstoy's last bedroom in Yasnaya Polyana. On the wall is a portrait of his daughter who died very young. *Opposite:* His washstand and, hanging from hooks on the wall, his daily dress of the last years: a peasant shirt, hat, and walking sticks. The portrait is of his wife, Sophie Behrs.

They carried him not to bury him;
They carried him down to crown him.

Grayer than granite,
More reddish than bronze,
Steaming like a locomotive,
The poet flourished here,
                              disheveled,
Who would not bow before votive lamps
But to the common spade.

The lilac at his doorstep burned . . .
A fountain of falling stars
                              soaked in sweat,
His back steamed
Like a loaf in the oven.

Now his house gapes, vacant,
Tenantless;
There is nobody in the dining room,
There is not a soul in Russia.

It is the way of the poet to search
For sanctuary. He goes hatless,
                              as people do in church,
Through the murmuring fields
To the birch grove and the oaks.

In his flight is his victory;
In his retreat, an ascent
To pastures and planets
Far from lying ornament.

Forests shed their crowns of leaves,
But powerfully underground
Roots twist and thrust
Like a gnarled hand.

> —ANDREI VOZNESENSKY
> *"Leaves and Roots,"*
> *translated by Stanley Kunitz*

Tolstoy's tomb in the park of Yasnaya Polyana. The writer was buried here, according to his wishes, in an anonymous grave.

Black woods behind the old house
In front a sloping field of oats;
Above a cloud curves in soft sky
Like a silver ball; centered
Against the cloud, beating with
Severe, painful clarity,
The wing of a wounded swan;
Below on the old wooden balcony
A young man with white hair,
His face the enigma of time
Like a portrait in an old medallion. . . .

—NIKOLAI ZABOLOTSKY
From "The Poet" (Boris Pasternak),
adapted by James Schevill
with Olga Carlisle

Boris Pasternak's house in Peredelkino. Most celebrated in the West for his novel *Doctor Zhivago*, most celebrated in Russia as one of its greatest poets, Pasternak lived the greater part of his life in this wooden house surrounded by a garden. Across from it are a field and a wooded hill, and, nearby, the railway station he celebrated in many of his poems. *Opposite:* Photographs of Pasternak on the desk of a friend.

Through the darkness, behind the gate
and into the fields the smell flows sweet
of sleepy herbs from the garden aisles
and hot shiny quartz amid twigs and snails. . . .

—BORIS PASTERNAK
From "The Mirror,"
adapted by Rose Styron
with Olga Carlisle

Opposite: The pond at Peredelkino. *Above:* The field in front of Paster-nak's house. *Pages 202–203:* On the hill, opposite the field, the writer lies buried in the cemetery, his tomb covered with visitors' offerings.

We were in Georgia. You can get this land
If hell is multiplied by paradise,
Bare indigence by tenderness, and if
A hothouse serves as pedestal for ice.

And then you'll know what subtle doses of
Success and labor, duty, mountain air
Make the right mixture with the earth and sky
For man to be the way we found him there.

So that he grew, in famine and defeat
And bondage, to this stature, without fault,
Becoming thus a model and a mold,
Something as stable and as plain as salt.

—BORIS PASTERNAK
From "Waves,"
translated by Babette Deutsch

Opposite: Georgian icon in the Museum of Fine Arts, Tbilisi.

Overleaf: Along the Georgian military highway near Mtskhet.

Georgia. Sixteenth-century fort and the Church of Anamuri on a hill above the Aragvy River. The perfect proportions of the church's single dome are typical of Georgian architecture.

Overleaf: Tbilisi. Faces of young Georgians, assembled to honor their poet Georgi Leonidze on the first anniversary of his death, at the open-air Pantheon for famous men of Georgia.

Georgian countrywomen in traditional dress.

Opposite: A Georgian toast in the classic manner. The toastmaster's drinking vessel is a polished horn.

Overleaf: In the house of the widow of the Georgian painter David Kakabadze. The abstractions hanging on the back wall were painted by the artist in the early 1920s during his stay in Paris. The three big canvases are by Niko Pirosmani, the distinguished primitive Georgian painter of the early twentieth century.

The photographs on this and the following pages were taken during the
Festival of the Grapes at the eleventh-century church of Alaverdi in the
Kaheti Valley. A small crowd, comprised mostly of older men and women,
spent three days of prayer, listening to music, dancing, and perpetuating
other age-old traditions. *Overleaf:* A photographer brought Cossack
costumes for some to pose in. *Pages 224–225:* An old man walks slowly
around the church to kiss each corner. Inside the church he stopped and
bowed down to the ground before lighting a candle in front of a metal
crucifix which replaced the destroyed altar.

Preceding pages: A baker's window with traditional round *kulichki.*

North Samarkand, in central Asia. The houses in this desertlike landscape are mostly made of mud bricks. Rows of tobacco leaves (the chief local product, along with silk, cotton, and carpets) are hung up to dry under the grass roofs. *Preceding pages:* In the same region, a family of Uzbeks during washday in the Chupan-Ata mountains.

Arise, O prophet, look and ponder:
Arise, charged with my will, and spurred!
As over roads and seas you wander,
Kindle men's hearts with this, my Word.

—ALEXANDER PUSHKIN
From "The Prophet,"
translated by Babette Deutsch

Opposite: Part of the immense Mosque of Bibi Khanum, named after one of Tamburlaine's wives. The ancient town was resurrected in the fourteenth century by Tamburlaine, who made it the capital of the state and built many palaces, gardens, and mosques. During his reign the new city became the center of the Moslem civilization of central Asia, and it remained so for nearly two centuries. *Above:* Tamburlaine's tomb (*center*) in the Gar Amir Mausoleum, Samarkand.

Overleaf: Uzbeks visiting the Mosque of the Living God, Shah Sindegh, built by Tamburlaine in honor of Kasim, nephew of Mohammed.

Samarkand. Portraits of politicians line walkway in the Park of Rest and Culture.

Opposite: The splendid building of the Tillakari Mosque in Rigistan, Samarkand's most famous square.

Overleaf: Tractor driver. He represents the newer element in the local population of Uzbeks and Tadzhiks. Many Russians evacuated from the North during World War II came south to Samarkand.

Pages 238–239: Steps with statues in the city's Park of Rest and Culture.

. . . And thou, Russia, art not thou, too, rushing headlong
like the fastest troika that is not to be outdistanced.
. . . What is the meaning of this awe-inspiring onrush?
. . . Russia, whither art thou speeding? Answer me!
She gives no answer. . . . Everything on earth is flying
past, and the other nations and states, eyeing her askance,
make way for her and draw aside. . . .

—NIKOLAI GOGOL
From Dead Souls,
translated by Constance Garnett

DATE DUE

OCT 6 '70			
JAN 5 '71			
OCT 18 '77			
APR 4	⌐		